D1341722

As many of our illustrated books have had pages removed, or pictures cut out we are now monitoring such books. Please fill in the following to indicate that this book was still complete when you returned it

| Name | Signature | Date Returned | Checked By |
|------|-----------|---------------|------------|
| | | | PC 10/06/10 ✗ |
| | Checked & all intact 26/11/10 PC | | |

# THOR

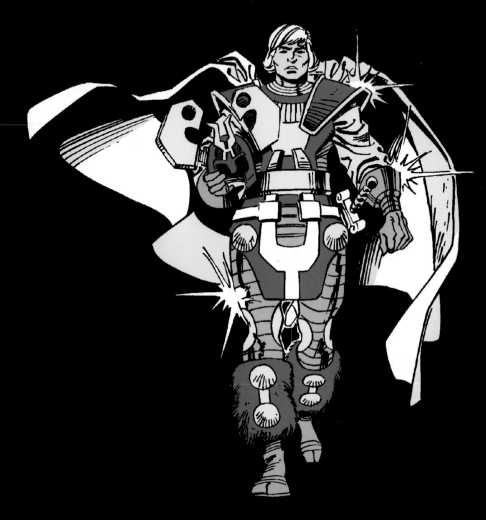

# BALDER THE BRAVE

SIMONSON · BUSCEMA

## THOR

### WRITER
# WALTER SIMONSON

### ARTISTS
# WALTER SIMONSON
# & SAL BUSCEMA

### COLORISTS
# CHRISTIE SCHEELE & PAUL BECTON

### LETTERER
# JOHN WORKMAN JR.

### EDITOR
# RALPH MACCHIO

### COVER ART
# WALTER SIMONSON

### FRONT COVER COLORS
# CHRIS SOTOMAYOR

### BACK COVER COLORS
# MIKE ATIYEH

**THOR: BALDER THE BRAVE PREMIERE.** Contains material originally published in magazine form as BALDER THE BRAVE #1-4 and THOR #360-362. First printing 2009. ISBN# 978-0-7851-3885-3. Published by MARVEL PUBLISHING, INC., a subsidiary of MARVEL ENTERTAINMENT, INC. OFFICE OF PUBLICATION: 417 5th Avenue, New York, NY 10016. Copyright © 1985, 1986 and 2009 Marvel Characters, Inc. All rights reserved. $24.99 per copy in the U.S. (GST #R127032852); Canadian Agreement #40668537. All characters featured in this issue and the distinctive names and likenesses thereof, and all related indicia are trademarks of Marvel Characters, Inc. No similarity between any of the names, characters, persons, and/or institutions in this magazine with those of any living or dead person or institution is intended, and any such similarity which may exist is purely coincidental. **Printed in China.** ALAN FINE, CEO Marvel Publishing Division and EVP & CMO Marvel Characters B.V.; DAN BUCKLEY, President of Publishing - Print & Digital Media; JIM SOKOLOWSKI, Chief Operating Officer; DAVID GABRIEL, SVP of Publishing Sales & Circulation; DAVID BOGART, SVP of Business Affairs & Talent Management; MICHAEL PASCIULLO, VP Merchandising & Communications; JIM O'KEEFE, VP of Operations & Logistics; DAN CARR, Executive Director of Publishing Technology; JUSTIN F. GABRIE, Director of Publishing & Editorial Operations; SUSAN CRESPI, Editorial Operations Manager; ALEX MORALES, Publishing Operations Manager; STAN LEE, Chairman Emeritus. For information regarding advertising in Marvel Comics or on Marvel.com, please contact Mitch Dane, Advertising Director, at mdane@marvel.com. For Marvel subscription inquiries, please call 800-217-9158.

10 9 8 7 6 5 4 3 2 1

COLLECTION EDITOR
**MARK D. BEAZLEY**

EDITORIAL ASSISTANT
**ALEX STARBUCK**

ASSISTANT EDITORS
**JOHN DENNING & CORY LEVINE**

EDITOR, SPECIAL PROJECTS
**JENNIFER GRÜNWALD**

SENIOR EDITOR, SPECIAL PROJECTS
**JEFF YOUNGQUIST**

PRODUCTION
**JERRON QUALITY COLOR &
JERRY KALINOWSKI**

RESEARCH
**JEPH YORK**

SENIOR VICE PRESIDENT OF SALES
**DAVID GABRIEL**

EDITOR IN CHIEF
**JOE QUESADA**

PUBLISHER
**DAN BUCKLEY**

EXECUTIVE PRODUCER
**ALAN FINE**

**BALDER THE BRAVE**

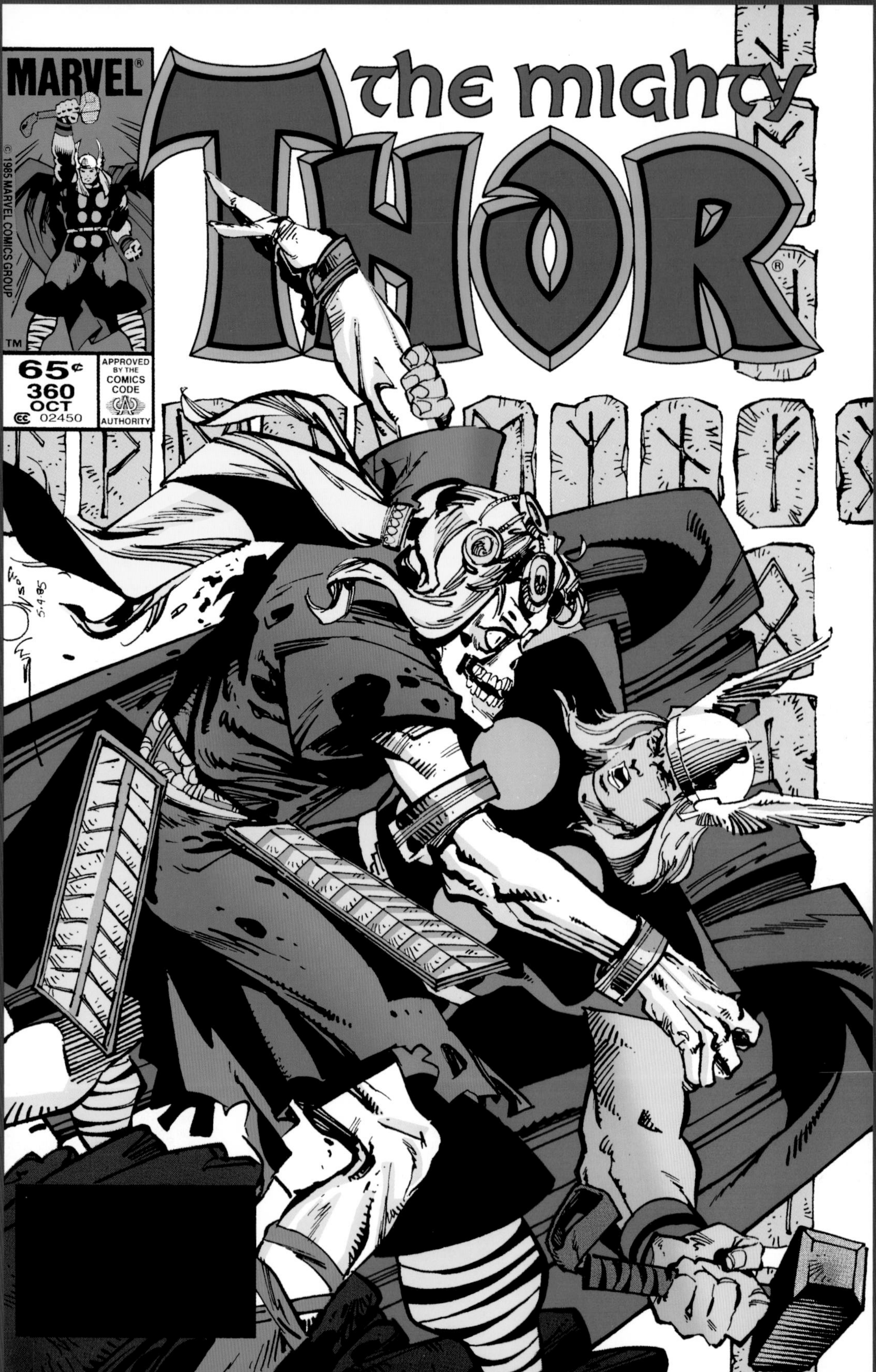
MARVEL®
© 1985 MARVEL COMICS GROUP
TM
65¢
360
OCT
02450
APPROVED BY THE COMICS CODE AUTHORITY
the mighty
THOR®

STAN LEE PRESENTS: the MIGHTY THOR

# INTO THE VALLEY OF DEATH!

WHEN THE FIGHTING IS OVER, THE WARRIORS COME HOME.

SINCE TIME IMMEMORIAL, THE VICTORIOUS SURVIVORS HAVE TAKEN THEIR TROPHYS AND THEIR WOUNDED AND RETURNED FROM WHENCE THEY CAME.

SO THE CHEERING WARRIORS OF THE GOLDEN REALM POUR FORTH FROM THE DIMENSIONAL RIFT THAT LEADS FROM EARTH TO ASGARD...

...AND FOR THE FIRST TIME IN DAYS BREATHE THE UNSULLIED AIR OF THE HOME OF THE MIGHTY NORSE GODS!

AT LAST!

TOO LONG HAVE WE TARRIED ON MIDGARD.*

*EARTH.

ART AND STORY: WALTER SIMONSON  LETTERING: JOHN WORKMAN, JR.  COLORS: CHRISTIE SCHEELE
EDITING: RALPH MACCHIO  EDITOR-IN-CHIEF: JIM SHOOTER

HAVE A CARE WITH THOSE CRATES, FELLOWS! SUCH MORTAL GOODS AS THESE HAVE NE'ER BEEN SEEN IN ASGARD BEFORE...

...AND THEY MAY CHANGE THE FACE OF VALHALLA BEFORE WE ARE THROUGH.

BUT *HURRY!* FOR THE GATEWAY BETWEEN THE WORLDS IS NEARLY *CLOSED* AND WE ARE THE LAST FEW TO LEAVE THE MORTAL REALM BEHIND!

HAROKIN CARRIES HIS CASKETS AS LOVINGLY AS A MOTHER HER NEWBORN BABE!

STILL, FANDRAL, HE IS A LARGE ENOUGH PRIZE FOR ANYONE.

AND WE HAVE ONLY *VOLSTAGG* TO SHOW FOR OUR STAY IN MIDGARD.

HOGUN, I'VE LOST MY GRIP UPON THE LION OF ASGARD'S ARM!

I, TOO, NO LONGER SENSE HIS MASSIVE GIRTH BEHIND US!

AND THE PORTAL SHRIEKS LIKE A *THOUSAND* DEMONS...

...THREATENING TO *CLOSE* BEHIND US AT ANY MOMENT!

MAKE WAY, YOU PUNY WARRIORS! THE LION OF ASGARD HATH RETURNED TO HIS DEN!

SPITHOOUMM!

VOLSTAGG!

LANDING WITH ALL THE GRACE OF A GAZELLE, I SEE...

...WHILE THE PORTAL CLOSES BEHIND US FOREVER!

IN TRUTH, VOLSTAGG, I THINK ONLY YOUR *MASSIVE* FORM PREVENTED THE PORTAL FROM CLOSING LONG BEFORE THIS.

SAY RATHER THAT THE *STRENGTH* OF VOLSTAGG'S NEARLY BOUNDLESS FRAME HATH ONCE AGAIN COME TO THE AID OF HIS BROTHERS!

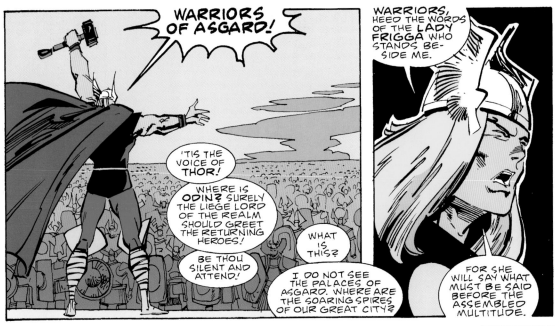

WARRIORS OF ASGARD!

'TIS THE VOICE OF THOR!

WHERE IS ODIN? SURELY THE LIEGE LORD OF THE REALM SHOULD GREET THE RETURNING HEROES!

BE THOU SILENT AND ATTEND!

WHAT IS THIS?

I DO NOT SEE THE PALACES OF ASGARD. WHERE ARE THE SOARING SPIRES OF OUR GREAT CITY?

WARRIORS, HEED THE WORDS OF THE LADY FRIGGA WHO STANDS BE-SIDE ME.

FOR SHE WILL SAY WHAT MUST BE SAID BEFORE THE ASSEMBLED MULTITUDE.

...AND ALL ACROSS THE PLAIN, A SILENCE FALLS MORE DEAFENING THAN THUNDER.

I SALUTE YOU, BRAVE WARRIORS. YOU HAVE WON A GREAT VICTORY FOR AS-GARD AND FOR ALL THE NINE WORLDS.

WITH-OUT YOUR VALOR AND YOUR COURAGE, ALL OUR HOPES WOULD HAVE BEEN IN VAIN.

BUT THOUGH YOU HAVE COME HOME, 'TIS NOT A HOME-COMING THAT ANY COULD HAVE FORESEEN.

THE WAR WITH SURTUR * HAS BEEN COSTLY. THE GREAT CITY OF ASGARD HAS NEARLY BEEN DE-STROYED.

AND YET THIS IS THE LEAST OF OUR LOSSES.

*ISSUES 350-353.

OH WARRIORS WEEPING FOR YOUR MATES WHO SHALL NOT RETURN FROM EARTH...

OH CHILDREN CRYING FOR YOUR FATHERS AND MOTHERS WHO SHALL NOT SEE ASGARD'S MAJESTY AGAIN...

...KNOW THAT FRIGGA SHARES YOUR GRIEF.

FOR ODIN, THE ALLFATHER, FELL WITH SURTUR INTO THE FIRES OF MUSPELHEIM.

YOUR LIEGE LORD...MY HUSBAND...HAS SACRIFICED HIMSELF THAT THE NINE WORLDS MIGHT LIVE!

7

BEHIND HIM HE HAS LEFT THE GREAT SCEPTER WHICH I HOLD BEFORE YOU NOW.

IN TIME, WE MUST CHOOSE A NEW RULER TO SIT IN ODIN'S HIGH SEAT AND TAKE UP THE SCEPTER'S CHALLENGE.

MY GRIEF OVER-COMES ME. I CAN SAY NO MORE.

BUT TODAY, LET US MOURN FOR ALL THOSE WHOSE PASSING HAS ALLOWED OUR EYES TO SEE ANOTHER SUNRISE.

...AND FOR THE SPACE OF SEVEN HEARTBEATS, NOT A SOUND IS HEARD ACROSS ALL THAT GREAT PLAIN.

ASGARDIANS! THE WAR IS **OVER!**

...SO SHOULD SHE CONTINUE AS CARETAKER OF THE REALM UN-TIL WE CAN ELECT A NEW LEADER.

BUT THERE IS **AN-OTHER** WRONG YET TO RIGHT!

I SAY THAT AS FRIGGA NOW HOLDS THE SCEPTER IN TRUST...

FOR THE ALLIES OF SURTUR HAVE LABORED MIGHTILY IN HIS CAUSE AND MUCH OF THEIR WORK REMAINS TO BE UNDONE!

FAR BELOW US, IN THE KINGDOM OF **HELA**, THE DEATH GODDESS, MOR-TAL SOULS LIE LAN-GUISHING IN BONDAGE...

...SENT THERE BY THE TREACH-EROUS WILES OF **MALEKITH** THE AC-CURSED *!

*THOR 345-348.

THESE INNOCENT VICTIMS OF AGELESS EVIL WERE SENT TO **HEL** WHEN THEY TASTED THE FOOD OF FAERIE...

...LEAVING BEHIND THEIR BODIES ON MIDGARD AS **SLAVES** TO THE DARK ELVES!

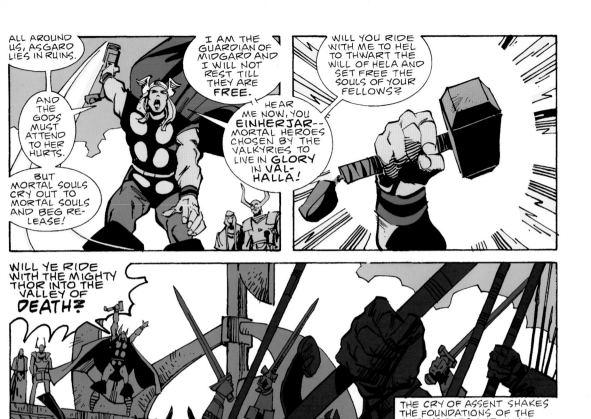

ALL AROUND US, ASGARD LIES IN RUINS.

AND THE GODS MUST ATTEND TO HER HURTS.

BUT MORTAL SOULS CRY OUT TO MORTAL SOULS AND BEG RELEASE!

I AM THE GUARDIAN OF MIDGARD AND I WILL NOT REST TILL THEY ARE FREE.

HEAR ME NOW, YOU EINHERJAR-- MORTAL HEROES CHOSEN BY THE VALKYRIES TO LIVE IN GLORY IN VALHALLA!

WILL YOU RIDE WITH ME TO HEL TO THWART THE WILL OF HELA AND SET FREE THE SOULS OF YOUR FELLOWS?

WILL YE RIDE WITH THE MIGHTY THOR INTO THE VALLEY OF DEATH?

THE CRY OF ASSENT SHAKES THE FOUNDATIONS OF THE NINE WORLDS AND IN HEL, EVEN HELA PAUSES A MOMENT AT THE ECHO.

YES, HAROKIN? WHAT WOULD THE LEADER OF THE EINHERJAR HAVE FROM THOR?

A MOMENT OF YOUR TIME, MY LORD.

I HAVE SOMETHING THAT I THINK YOU SHOULD SEE.

WHILE WE WERE ON MIDGARD, I HAD SOME OPPORTUNITY TO OBSERVE THE FIGHTING STYLES OF OUR MORTAL ALLIES.

AND I FOUND THEIR WEAPONS MOST INTERESTING.

SOME JUDICIOUS HORSETRADING HAS ENABLED ME TO RETURN TO ASGARD WITH A LARGE SAMPLING OF MORTAL INGENUITY.

MY MEN HAVE ALREADY BEGUN TO MASTER THESE STRANGE AND WONDERFUL WEAPONS, MY LORD.

IN TRUTH I HAD NOT ANTICIPATED SUCH EARLY USEFULNESS...

...BUT SAY THE WORD, AND WE'LL SHOW HELA TEETH OF STEEL SHE NEVER DREAMED EXISTED.

I SOMETIMES THINK, HAROKIN, THAT THE PRESCIENCE OF MORTALS FREQUENTLY EXCEEDS THAT OF THE GODS.

9

A SHORT TIME LATER...

I AM DEPENDING UPON YOU, AGNAR.

SEEK OUT **BALDER** IN THE REALM OF THE **NORN QUEEN** AND TELL HIM THAT I HAVE **NEED** OF HIM HERE IN ASGARD.

I SHALL NOT FAIL YOU, MY LORD.*

FOR ONLY **HE** KNOWS THE WAY **HOME** FROM THE DISMAL HALLS OF DEATH.

BUT CAN YOU BE SURE YOU WILL NOT FAIL **HIM**, THOR?

AS I HAVE FAILED YOU, SIF?

*THE RESULTS OF AGNAR'S MISSION CAN BE EXPLORED IN DETAIL IN **BALDER THE BRAVE** No. 1-- ON SALE AUGUST.

I MEAN, MY LORD, THAT WHATEVER YOUR INTENTIONS, YOU...

...YOU MAY YET DISAPPOINT THOSE WHO **FOLLOW** YOU.

OR **LOVE** ME?

I... HAVE **NEVER** SAID SO, MY LORD.

SOME DECLARATIONS, SIF, ARE NOT SPOKEN.

AND IF BEGGING COULD EARN YOUR FORGIVENESS, MY LADY, I WOULD ABASE MYSELF UTTERLY.

I HAVE NEVER ASKED THAT OF YOU.

NOR FORGIVEN ME FOR STRIKING YOU.*

*LAST ISSUE.

PERFECTION IS NOT GIVEN EVEN TO THE GODS OF ASGARD, MY LADY.

AND WITHOUT PERFECTION, THERE IS ALWAYS FAILURE.

I WOULD GIVE ANYTHING TO BE MADE PERFECT IN YOUR EYES AGAIN.

SO IF YOU WILL EXCUSE ME, MY LADY, I WILL TROUBLE YOU NO LONGER WITH MY PRESENCE.

BUT EVEN THE POWER OF MY FATHER ODIN COULD NOT UNDO WHAT HAS BEEN DONE.

THOR SEEMS GRIMMER THAN IS HIS WONT.

BUT NEVER DOUBT THAT HE LOVES YOU, SISTER.

I CANNOT IMAGINE, HEIMDALL, THAT IF HE **TRULY** LOVED ME, HE WOULD HAVE STRUCK ME UNDER ANY CIRCUMSTANCES.

WHAT TINY IMAGINATIONS IMMORTALS HAVE.

FLAWED HE MAY BE AND DEEPLY HURT BY THE LOSS OF HIS FATHER.

YET PERHAPS **NO** WOUND GOES DEEPER THAN THIS ONE.

HE **STRUCK** ME, HEIMDALL! HOW CAN I **EVER** FORGET THAT?

NO ONE HAS ASKED YOU TO. BUT IS IT SO DIFFICULT A THING TO FORGIVE?

SMALL WONDER HE SEEKS THE PITS OF HEL SO EAGERLY.

HEIMDALL?

'TIS THE ENCHANTRESS!

HEIMDALL, I HAVE BEEN SEARCHING FOR YOU EVERYWHERE.

PLEASE WALK WITH ME. I'VE SOMETHING TO DISCUSS WITH YOU. IF YOU'LL FORGIVE US, SIF?

I WAS JUST LEAVING. I HAVE SAID WHAT I HAD TO SAY HERE.

AT THE EDGE OF ASGARD, NESTLED AGAINST THE MOUNTAIN'S ROOTS STAND THE HALLS OF ODIN...

...AND AS THE DAY DRAWS ON, A SINGLE VISITOR ENTERS THE GREAT GATEWAY.

I HAVE BEEN WAITING FOR YOU, MY SON. EVER SINCE I HEARD YOU SPEAK OF HEL, I KNEW YOU WOULD COME.

I DOUBT THAT HE IS IN HELA'S WAITING ARMS, THOR.

YOUR FATHER WAS EVER TRUE TO ME IN HIS HEART.

ODIN WOULD NOT HAVE DESERTED ME FOR HER.

HELA WOULD NOT HAVE ASKED HIS PERMISSION, MOTHER.

AND BY NOW, SHE MAY HAVE FOUND HIS SHADE AND LURED IT WITHIN HER KINGDOM.

I MUST KNOW.

AND THE MORTALS MUST BE FREED.

BUT ONLY THE DEAD KNOW THE WAY TO HEL.

SO YOU HAVE COME TO TEST THE POWER OF ODIN'S RUNES. DO NOT DO THIS THING, MY SON.

THERE ARE SOME MAGICKS THAT EVEN ODIN FEARED TO WORK.

LET THE PATH TO DEATH REMAIN UNTRODDEN BY THE LIVING.

SINCE THAT ROAD IS KNOWN ONLY TO THE DEAD, MOTHER...

...THEN I SHALL ASK THE DEAD TO SHOW ME ITS SECRET.

AND WHEN I HOLD THE RUNES OF MY FATHER IN MY HAND, THEY WILL ANSWER ME.

12

...EVEN THE FUTURE...

...OR THE PAST.

THE CASKET GROWS HEAVIER AND HEAVIER THE HIGHER I CLIMB...

AND THE DEAD BELONG TO THE PAST.

FAR ABOVE ASGARD, TOWERING OVER ALL THE REALM STANDS THE **HLIDSKJALF,** THE HIGH SEAT...

...WHERE ONCE ODIN SAT AND WATCHED THE WORKINGS OF THE NINE WORLDS.

FROM THE HIGH SEAT, IT IS SAID THAT A GOD CAN SEE ALL THINGS...

...BUT THERE IS **NO** WEIGHT... TOO GREAT TO KEEP ME ...FROM ACHIEVING THE SUMMIT.

...AND NO RISK I WOULD NOT DARE TO ACHIEVE MY GOAL!

FATHER, IF YOU ARE THERE, I SHALL FIND YOU!

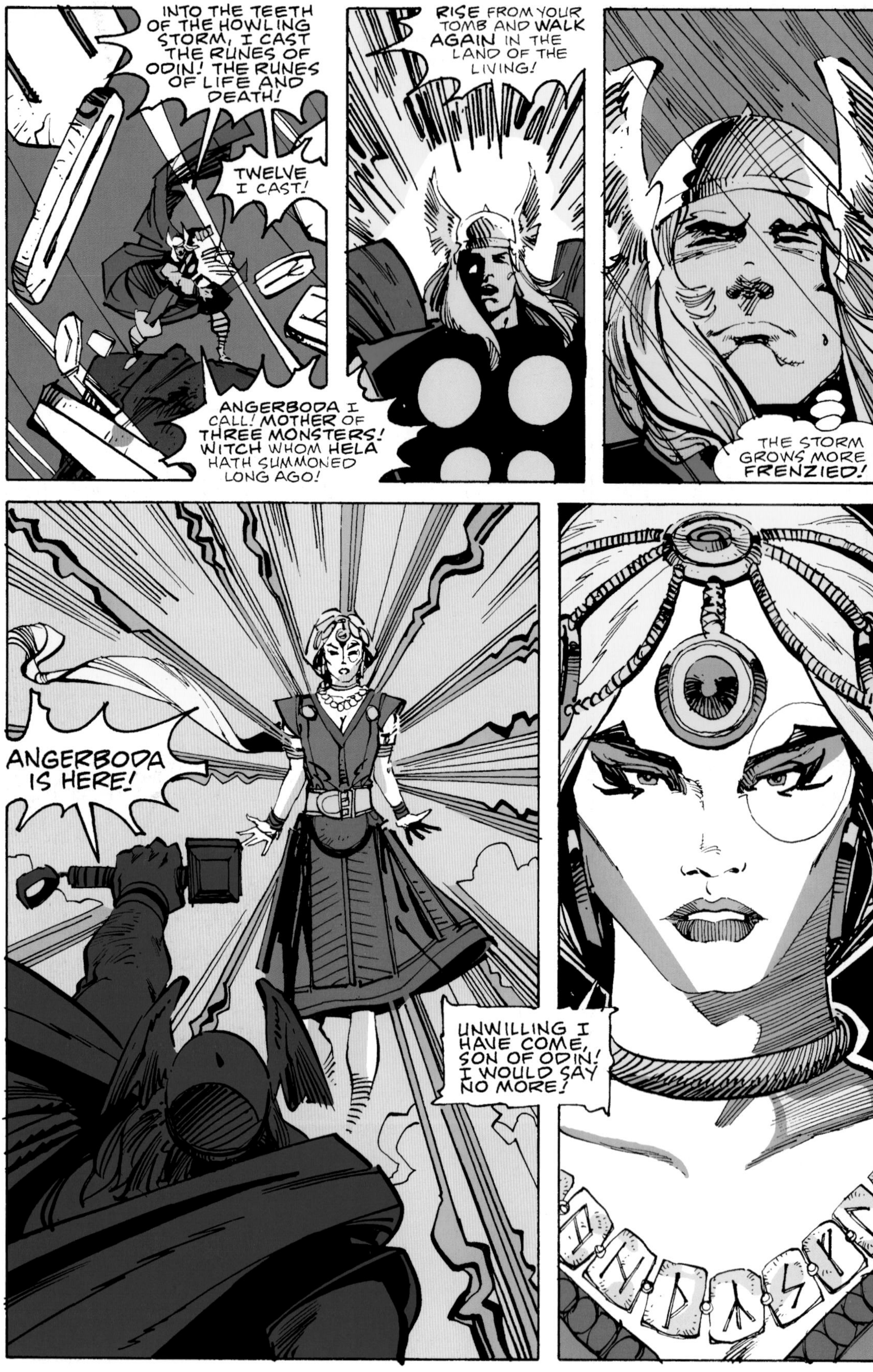
INTO THE TEETH OF THE HOWLING STORM, I CAST THE RUNES OF ODIN! THE RUNES OF LIFE AND DEATH!
TWELVE I CAST!
ANGERBODA I CALL! MOTHER OF THREE MONSTERS! WITCH WHOM HELA HATH SUMMONED LONG AGO!
RISE FROM YOUR TOMB AND WALK AGAIN IN THE LAND OF THE LIVING!
THE STORM GROWS MORE FRENZIED!
ANGERBODA IS HERE!
UNWILLING I HAVE COME, SON OF ODIN! I WOULD SAY NO MORE!

SPEAK, WITCH, OF THE **ROAD** TO **HEL.** SPEAK OF THE ROAD THAT A LIVING MAN MIGHT TREAD!

UNWILLING I SHALL SPEAK! I WOULD SAY NO MORE!

THE **RUNES** ABOUT YOUR NECK MAKE YOU **MINE** TO COMMAND! SPEAK, WITCH, OF THE ROAD TO HEL.

SEEK IN THE SHADOWS OF THE HEL-HOUND, **GARM,** FOR THE ENTRANCE!

BLACK THE ENTRANCE; BLACKER STILL THE JOURNEY.

NINE DAYS RIDE WILL BRING YOU TO THE RIVER **GJOLL** AND THE BRIDGE **GJALLERBRU!**

MODGUD GUARDS THE BRIDGE AND **HELGATE** LIES BEYOND IT.

UNWILLING I HAVE SPOKEN! I WOULD SAY NO MORE!

AND I HAVE SEEN WHAT NO LIVING BEING SHOULD SEE.

RETURN, ANGERBODA, TO YOUR GRAVE AND LEAVE THE LAND OF LIFE. I HAVE LEARNED WHAT I MUST KNOW AND I RELEASE YOU!

15

I SHALL RETURN TO HEL, MIGHTY THOR, BUT **NOT** ALONE!

FOR IF **YOU** WOULD TRAVEL THE ROAD TO DEATH, I CAN SHOW YOU A **QUICKER** WAY TO FIND IT!

EMBRACE ME, FOOL!

AND FALL WITH ME TO THY **DOOM!** HELA SHALL GREET THE SON OF ODIN AT LAST!

HER STRENGTH IS **UNBE-LIEV-ABLE!**

SHE HAS SEALED MY LIPS! I CANNOT SPEAK TO COMMAND HER!

AND IN ANOTHER MOMENT, I SHALL JOIN HER ON THE HELWAY...

...BUT NO LONGER AS A **LIVING BEING!**

THE RUNES BROUGHT HER TO THIS WORLD!

THEN LET THEM SEND HER BACK TO **HEL!!**

SHATTER!

16

AAAIEEEEEEEEEEEEEE!!!

IT IS **OVER**. ANGERBODA HAS RETURNED TO THE REALM OF DEATH!

AND I MUST RETURN THE RUNES TO MY FATHER'S HALL.

BUT I FEEL AS THOUGH THE STORMCLOUDS HAVE SETTLED UPON MY HEART...

...AND DIRE FORE- BODINGS ECHO IN MY SOUL THIS NIGHT!

MEANWHILE, FAR BELOW THE HIGH SEAT, IN THE GREEN WOODS NOT FAR FROM ASGARD...

THAT MAY BE, AMORA, BUT WHAT OF YOUR NOISY FRIEND WHO FOL- LOWS US?

WHAT?

THE EX- ECUTIONER, I BELIEVE?

FOR LO, THESE MANY YEARS, HEIMDALL, YOU HAVE STRAYED NOT A FOOT FROM THE RAINBOW BRIDGE.

A FAITHFUL GUARD AND GUARDIAN

BUT NOW THAT THE BRIDGE HAS BEEN DESTROYED, I THINK THE TIME HAS COME THAT WE SHOULD KNOW EACH OTHER BETTER.

ENCHANTRESS! AT **LAST!** I HAVE BEEN LOOKING ACROSS ALL OF ASGARD FOR YOU!

HOW INOP- PORTUNE OF YOU TO FIND ME AT THIS MOMENT, SKURGE!

WOULD YOU EXCUSE US FOR A MOMENT, HEIMDALL?

COME SKURGE, LET US RETIRE PRIVATELY.

AND A SIMPLE SPELL SHALL INSURE THAT HEIMDALL DOES NOT SEE OR OVERHEAR WHAT FOLLOWS.

AMORA, I HAD TO FIND YOU WHEN I CAME BACK TO ASGARD! YOU LEFT ME **ALONE** ON EARTH.

I COULDN'T STAND TO BE WITHOUT YOU FOR SO LONG!

PERHAPS 'TIS TIME YOU LEARNED TO **STAND** UPON YOUR OWN TWO FEET AGAIN.

WHA--!!

MY FEET! MY **LEGS**! THEY-- MMPHH!!

EXACTLY! THEY'VE BECOME TREE TRUNKS, ROOTING YOU TO THE GROUND HERE IN THE FOREST!

AND THIS **SPELL OF SILENCE** WILL KEEP YOU QUIET WHILE HEIMDALL AND I CONTINUE ON OUR WAY.

THE SPELLS WILL EXPIRE... EVENTUALLY.

BUT DO **NOT** TROUBLE ME AGAIN, SKURGE, WHEN I AM WITH ANOTHER MAN.

OR IT WILL BE THE WORSE FOR YOU.

YOUR FRIEND, AMORA?

HAS DEPARTED FOR ANOTHER PART OF THE FOREST.

FORGET HIM. I HAVE.

18

THE DAYS PASS AND THE REPAIR OF THE GOLDEN CITY CONTINUES DAY AND NIGHT...

...AS DO THE PREPARATIONS FOR THOR'S FORTHCOMING JOURNEY WITH THE HEROES OF VALHALLA...

...UNTIL...

THAT CLOUD OF DUST BELOW THE HORIZON! AT LAST!

THE WAITING IS OVER!

BALDER, MY FRIEND, WHO IS MORE THAN A BROTHER TO ME!

WELCOME HOME!

THOR!

LET ME EMBRACE THEE, BRAVE ONE!

NEVER HAVE I SEEN THEE LOOK BETTER!

MY THANKS, AGNAR, FOR BRINGING HOME THE LIGHT OF ASGARD!

19

AGNAR HAS TOLD YOU WHAT I PROPOSE TO DO?

WHAT SAYEST THOU?

HE HAS, NOBLE THOR. AND THE THOUGHT TO RESCUE THESE LOST MORTALS FROM HEL ONLY DOES YOU HONOR.

BUT IN TRUTH, I WONDER IF YOU **KNOW** WHAT YOU ARE ASKING OF THE EINHERJAR, OF ME, AND OF **YOURSELF.**

**MUCH** DID I TELL VOLSTAGG OF MY SOJOURN IN HEL, THOR*...BUT EVEN FROM HIM I HELD BACK THE LAST HORROR.

*THOR 338/339.

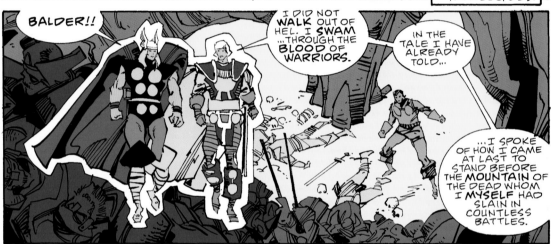

BALDER!!

I DID NOT **WALK** OUT OF HEL. I **SWAM** ...THROUGH THE **BLOOD OF WARRIORS.**

IN THE TALE I HAVE ALREADY TOLD...

...I SPOKE OF HOW I CAME AT LAST TO STAND BEFORE THE **MOUNTAIN** OF THE DEAD WHOM I **MYSELF** HAD SLAIN IN COUNTLESS BATTLES.

I DID NOT SPEAK OF HELA, OR HOW I FOUND HER WAITING FOR ME THERE.

WELCOME, BALDER. LONG HAVE I AWAITED YOUR COMING.

AND LONGER STILL YOU HAVE TO WAIT.

FOR THOUGH MY SPIRIT STANDS BEFORE YOU, MY BODY STILL LIES IN ASGARD, PROTECTED BY THE SPELL OF ODIN*.

AND AS LONG AS ASGARD STANDS, I SHALL NOT TRULY BE THINE!

WELL SAID, BRAVE ONE. BUT IF YOUR WANDERING SPIRIT SHOULD PERISH WITHIN MY KINGDOM...

...NOT EVEN **ODIN'S SPELLS** WILL CALL YOU BACK TO ASGARD.

* WAY BACK IN THOR 275 !!

20

"BUT FOR ONE SO BEAUTIFUL, EVEN DEATH MUST BE FAIR.

THERE, BRAVE ONE, LIES THE PATH FROM DARKNESS.

IF YOU BUT CLIMB THAT WINDING ROAD, BALDER SHALL SEE THE SUN AGAIN!

BUT BEFORE YOU GO, I HAVE GATHERED SOME OLD FRIENDS WHO WOULD LIKE TO GREET YOU.

THEY HAVE WAITED A LONG TIME TO SEE THEIR FORMER BATTLE COMPANION...

...AND JOYFULLY DO THEY LONG TO TASTE THY SHINING STEEL AGAIN!

COME, BALDER, AND WELCOME THY FORMER SWORD-MATES!

COME, BALDER, AND PLAY THE GAME OF DEATH!

HER LAUGHTER ECHOED THROUGHOUT THAT FORSAKEN PLACE!

THERE WAS NO OTHER SOUND.

...AND BECOME NO MORE THAN THE FOES I HAD ONCE SLAIN...

AND I KNEW THEN THAT TO FALL TO THE WEAPONS OF THE WARRIORS BEFORE ME WAS TO SURRENDER TO HELA...

...A MINDLESS, WILLLESS SLAVE TO THE GODDESS OF THE UNDERWORLD.

AND SO I FOUGHT.

I FOUGHT AS I HAVE NEVER FOUGHT BEFORE -- AND HOPED NEVER TO FIGHT AGAIN.

TIME HAD NO MEANING IN THAT TERRIBLE PLACE...

...AND I DO NOT KNOW HOW LONG THE BATTLE RAGED...

...OR HOW MANY BITTER TEARS I SHED.

I KNOW ONLY THAT IN THE END, I STRODE OUT OF HEL ALIVE.

MY HAIR WAS WHITE...

...AND I HAD SLAIN MY TEN THOUSANDS...

...AGAIN!

THIS IS WHAT YOU ASK OF EVERY HERO WHO RIDES WITH YOU.

HELA SHALL BE WAITING EAGERLY TO GREET THE MEN WHO HAVE DONE SO MUCH TO FILL HER EMPTY HALLS.

I HAVE GIVEN MY WORD, BALDER. I WILL GO INTO HEL IF I HAVE TO GO ALONE.

I KNEW YOUR ANSWER, MY DEAREST FRIEND. AND ONE AT LEAST SHALL RIDE WITH YOU INTO THE DARKNESS.

THEN LET THE HORDES OF HEL BEWARE.

22

I HAVE COME TO SAY GOODBYE, MOTHER. LET THE CALL GO OUT TO SUMMON ALL LOYAL ASGARDIANS TO THE ALTHING!

THE ASSEMBLY SHALL MEET WHEN WE RETURN AND THEN SHALL ALL ASGARDIANS DECIDE WHO WILL HOLD THE SCEPTER OF ODIN.

WE WILL LEAVE TO-NIGHT.

SHE WILL YIELD UP THE MORTALS, FRIGGA! OR NEVER AGAIN SHALL I SEE THE GOLDEN ROOFS OF ASGARD.

IF ALL YOU FIND IN HEL ARE THE MORTALS, I FEAR YOU WILL NOT BE SATISFIED, THOR.

THENCE-FORTH, THE DARK SHALL BE OUR CLOAK UNTIL WE STAND BEFORE HELA HERSELF.

OH, MY POOR BOY, I FEAR THAT EVEN HELA SHALL NOT BE ABLE TO GIVE YOU WHAT YOU SEEK.

THEN SO BE IT. MAY THE GOLDEN REALM ENDURE AS LONG AS THE NINE WORLDS...

...AND MAY THE SCEPTER OF MY FATHER KEEP YOU AND GUARD YOU FROM HARM TILL I RETURN.

IF YOU RETURN!

SIF!

I SEE THAT YOU TWO HAVE SOMETHING TO SAY TO EACH OTHER. IF YOU WILL EXCUSE ME...?

WHAT IS IT YOU WANT, SIF? I CAN SEE THAT MY VERY PRESENCE CAUSES YOU PAIN.

WHY DO YOU SEEK ME OUT?

I WANT TO KNOW-- WHY YOU STRUCK ME. AND WHY YOU LET ME GO WITH BETA RAY BILL.

LOVE IS THE ANSWER TO BOTH QUESTIONS, SIF.

I COULD NOT HOLD YOU FROM GOING WITH BILL WHEN HE AND HIS QUEST WERE WHAT YOU NEEDED MOST.

AND MY LOVE FOR LORELEI WAS SO ALL-CONSUMING, SO ALL-ENVELOPING THAT I WOULD HAVE DONE ANYTHING FOR IT.

BUT THAT LOVE WAS FALSE; A SPELL WROUGHT OF MAGIC!

PERHAPS THAT MADE IT ALL THE MORE POTENT.

NOW, LIKE ALL MAGIC, IT HAS FADED INTO NOTHING BUT THE CONSEQUENCES REMAIN.

ARE YOU CERTAIN THERE IS NOT ANOTHER ANSWER? THAT IN FACT YOU MAY NEVER HAVE LOVED ME TRULY?

WHAT CAN I ANSWER TO THAT?

YOU WOULD HAVE CERTAINTY WHEN ALL I SEE NOW IS ILLUSION.

WHEN ODIN VANISHED, HE TOOK ALL CERTAINTY WITH HIM.

BUT THIS I TRULY KNOW, I LOVED THE LADY SIF AS I HAVE NEVER LOVED ANOTHER.

WILL YOU CALL BILL TO THE ALTHING?

FOR WHAT REASON? HE IS NO ASGARDIAN.

HE IS ODIN'S **LAST**, PERHAPS HIS **GREATEST** WORK. AS **WORTHY** AS THE MIGHTY THOR HIMSELF!

ANOTHER CERTAINTY, MY LADY?

VERY WELL. SUMMON BILL BACK FROM EARTH IF YOU DESIRE. BUT REMEMBER WHAT I AM LEARNING NOW...

...MAGIC, EVEN MY FATHER'S, MAY ONLY BE ILLUSION IN THE END. AND WE LIVE WITH THE CONSEQUENCES.

NOW IF YOU WILL PARDON ME...

..."THE LONGER WE DELAY, THE LONGER INNOCENTS MUST LANGUISH IN HEL.

DID YOU REALLY HOPE HE WOULD ANSWER SUCH QUESTIONS?

I...I WANTED TO HEAR SOMETHING ELSE.

SIF, MY FOSTER-SON IS FALLABLE, AS ARE ALL OF US. AND HE HAS LOST HIS FATHER.

YET HEED THIS ONE WORD--BETA RAY BILL IS A WORTHY HERO IN-DEED.

BUT BEWARE --HE IS A **MORTAL** AND IN THE END, MORTALS MAY BE AS ILLUSORY AS MAGIC.

DO NOT JUDGE HIM TOO HARSHLY-- THE POWER OF LOKI'S ENCHANTMENTS IS BEYOND QUESTION.

THOR!

WHAT DO YOU WANT, SKURGE? I AM IN NO MOOD FOR TRIFLES JUST NOW.

NOR AM I, THOR.

I WANT TO RIDE WITH YOU INTO HEL!

YOU WOULD NOT REGRET IT.' 'TIS SOMETHING I NEED TO DO.

I THINK PERHAPS THAT WE SHARE THE SAME NEED, EXECUTIONER.

VERY WELL. WE LEAVE WITHIN THE HOUR.

AND LESS THAN AN HOUR LATER...

ALL IS READY, MY FRIEND.

I THINK THE LONG NIGHT HAS BEGUN.

HOW GOES IT, BALDER?

THE EIN-HERJAR ARE IMPATIENT, MY LORD!

THEN FOLLOW ME, YOU HEROES...

...AND LET THE HUNT BEGIN!

FOR HELA BECKONS AND THE HEL-HOUND GARM AWAITS!

NEXT: *THE QUICK AND THE DEAD!*
OR *HEL IS FOR HEROES!!*

The tale begins here – THE MIGHTY THOR #360 –
as Thor and Balder journey to the depths
of Hela's realm . . . and it continues in . . .

# BALDER
## THE BRAVE

The first issue in a four-part limited series that will
decide the fate of Balder, the Norns, and the
golden realm of Asgard itself!

**On sale in August.**

AND DON'T FORGET **THE RAVEN BANNER** Marvel's newest Graphic Novel.
A tale of heroism and tragedy from Asgard's misty past.
In book stores and comics specialty stores everywhere.

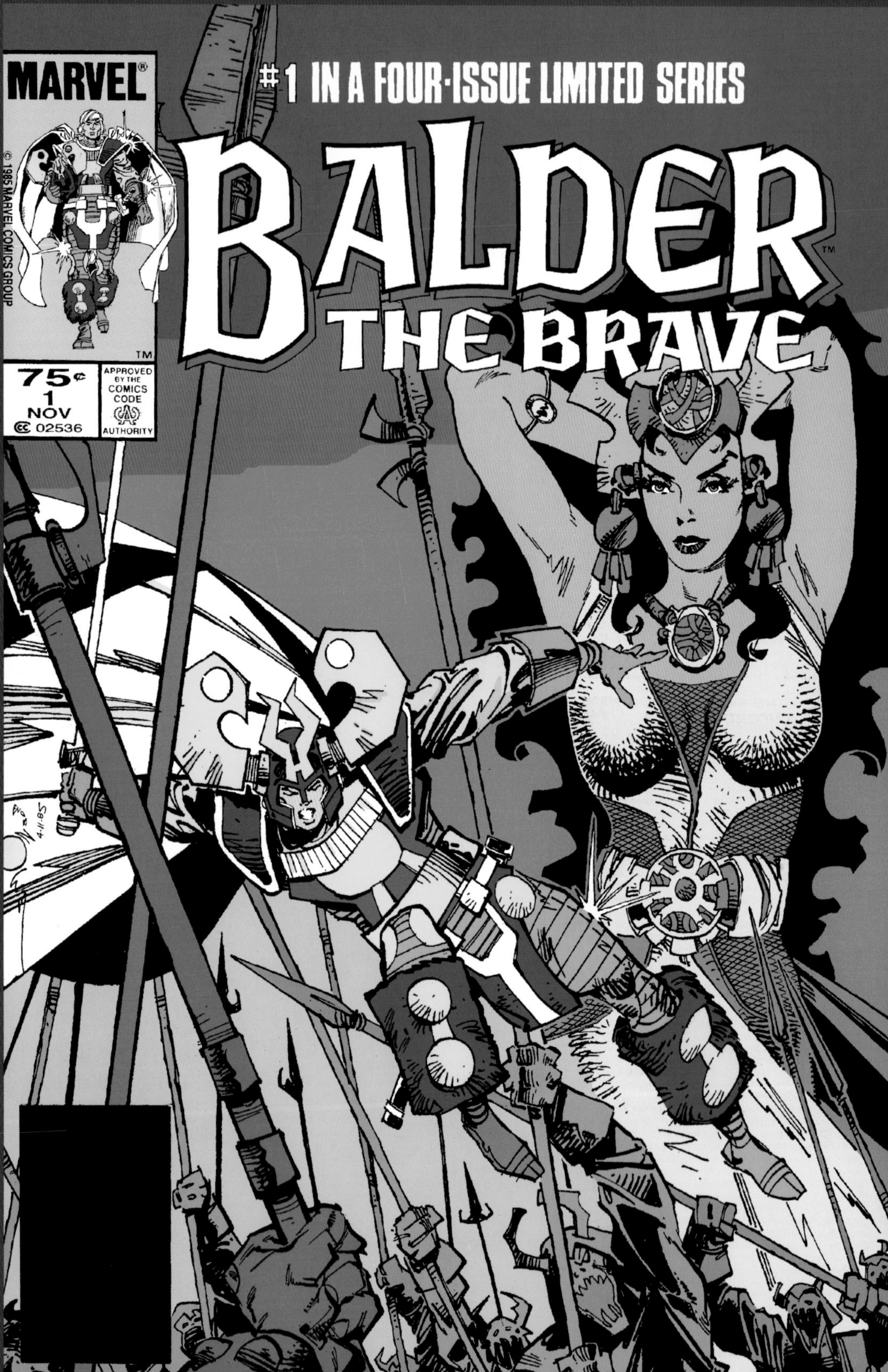
MARVEL®
#1 IN A FOUR-ISSUE LIMITED SERIES
BALDER™
THE BRAVE
© 1985 MARVEL COMICS GROUP
TM
75¢
1
NOV
CC 02536
APPROVED BY THE COMICS CODE AUTHORITY

# PROLOGUE:

THE LEGENDS TELL OF **ASGARD**, AND OF THE MIGHTY **NORSE GODS** WHO DWELT THEREIN. AND THEY SAY THAT IN THE DEEPS OF TIME, THE LORD **FREY**, GOD OF THE FERTILE EARTH, GAZED UPON THE LOVELINESS OF **GERD**...

...AND SWORE THAT SHE SHOULD BE HIS WIFE.

SO FREY CALLED HIS CHILDHOOD FRIEND, **SKIRNIR**, TO HIS SIDE AND BADE HIM RIDE TO GERD AND WOO HER FOR HIM.

AND HE GAVE SKIRNIR HIS **MAGIC SWORD** IN TOKEN OF HIS EARNEST.

A SWORD THAT MADE ITS WIELDER **UNCONQUERABLE**...

...FOR THE SHINING BLADE FOUGHT OF ITS OWN ACCORD AND NO SUBSTANCE COULD WITHSTAND ITS CUTTING EDGE.

SKIRNIR WON THE HAND OF GERD FOR FREY AND KEPT THE MAGIC SWORD.

BUT THOUGH THE SWORD MADE ITS WEARER UNCONQUERABLE IN BATTLE...

...IT DID **NOT** BESTOW PROTECTION AGAINST CUNNING AND SUBTLETY.

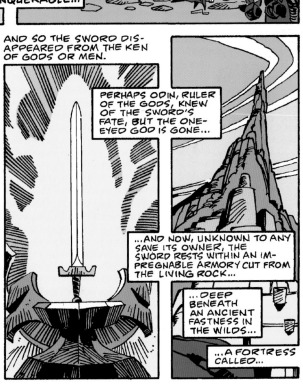

AND SO THE SWORD DISAPPEARED FROM THE KEN OF GODS OR MEN.

PERHAPS ODIN, RULER OF THE GODS, KNEW OF THE SWORD'S FATE, BUT THE ONE-EYED GOD IS GONE...

...AND NOW, UNKNOWN TO ANY SAVE ITS OWNER, THE SWORD RESTS WITHIN AN IMPREGNABLE ARMORY CUT FROM THE LIVING ROCK...

...DEEP BENEATH AN ANCIENT FASTNESS IN THE WILDS...

...A FORTRESS CALLED...

...THE NORN QUEEN!

the SWORD of FREY

PATIENCE, LITTLE FRIEND. THERE IS PLENTY FOR ALL AND A GENTLEMAN ALWAYS WAITS FOR THE LADY.

DO YOU KNOW HOW LONG, BRAVE BALDER, IT HAS BEEN SINCE THE BIRDS HAVE DEIGNED TO PERCH ATOP MY AERIE AND SING THEIR SONGS OF LOVE?

WRITTEN BY WALTER SIMONSON | ILLUSTRATED BY SAL BUSCEMA | LETTERED BY JOHN WORKMAN, JR. | COLORED BY PAUL BECTON | EDITED BY RALPH MACCHIO | EDITOR IN CHIEF JIM SHOOTER

MAYHAP I HOLD THE BIRDSEED IN A FRIENDLIER MANNER THAN THEE.

'TIS A LONG TIME SINCE I HELD BIRDSEED FOR ANY WINGED CREATURE.

THEN NO DOUBT YOU LACK THE PRACTICE AT THIS SIMPLE SKILL.

SKREEE! SKREEEE!

AND WILL BIRDSEED SUFFICE FOR THIS REGAL FOWL?

HO, BIG FELLOW.

HOW IS IT WITH YOU, WHITEFACE, FATHER OF EAGLES? HOW FARES THE REALM ETERNAL?

HOW IS IT, BALDER, THAT THE BIRDS DO NOT COME CLOSE TO MY HAND?

PERHAPS THE BIRDS ARE NO ONE'S FOOLS, KARNILLA.

AND WHAT PRAY TELL, MY NOBLE WARRIOR, DOES THAT MAKE YOU?

WHAT?

SKREEE! SKREEEEK!

31

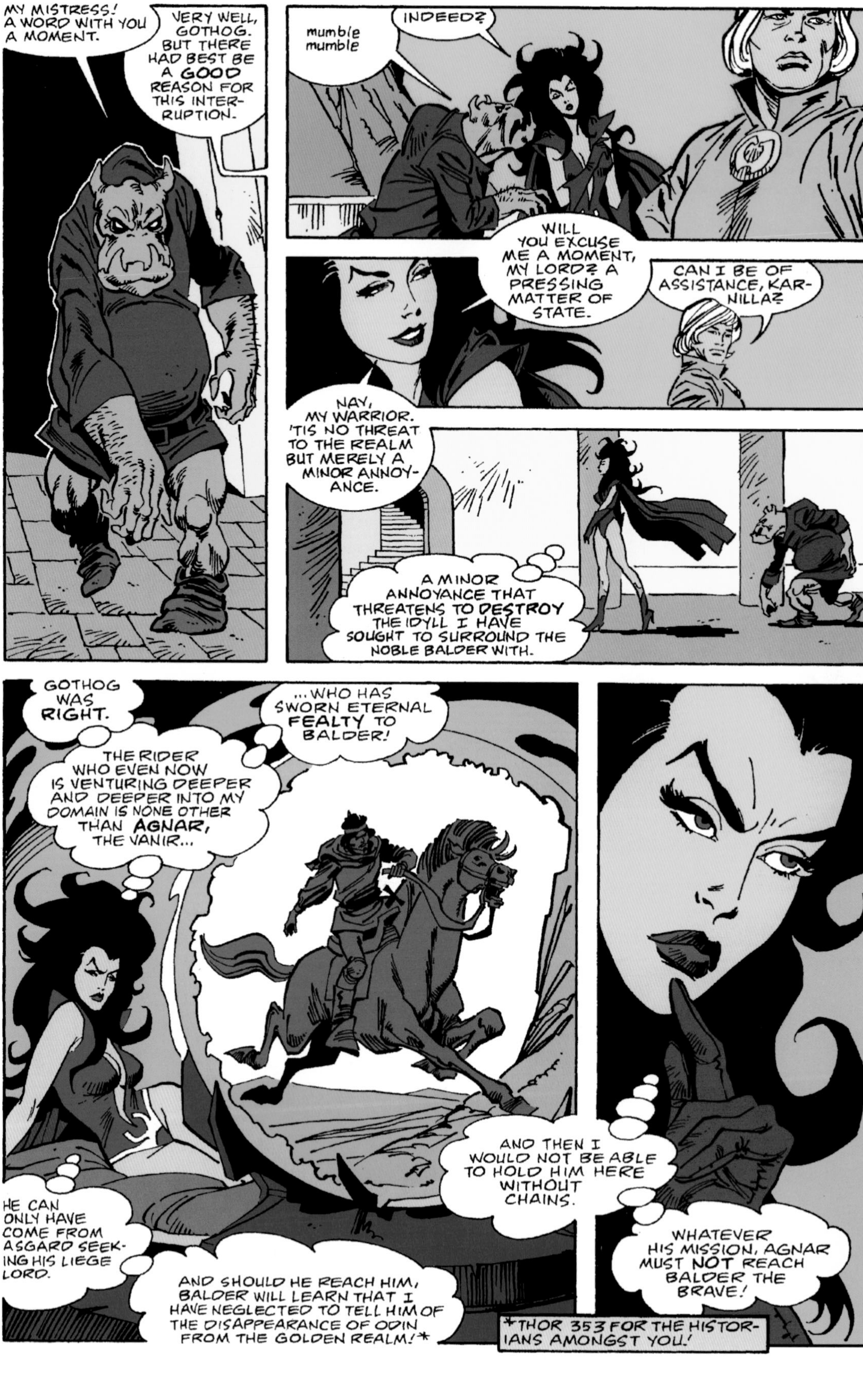
MY MISTRESS! A WORD WITH YOU A MOMENT.
VERY WELL, GOTHOG. BUT THERE HAD BEST BE A GOOD REASON FOR THIS INTERRUPTION.
mumble mumble
INDEED?
WILL YOU EXCUSE ME A MOMENT, MY LORD? A PRESSING MATTER OF STATE.
CAN I BE OF ASSISTANCE, KARNILLA?
NAY, MY WARRIOR. 'TIS NO THREAT TO THE REALM BUT MERELY A MINOR ANNOYANCE.
A MINOR ANNOYANCE THAT THREATENS TO DESTROY THE IDYLL I HAVE SOUGHT TO SURROUND THE NOBLE BALDER WITH.
GOTHOG WAS RIGHT.
THE RIDER WHO EVEN NOW IS VENTURING DEEPER AND DEEPER INTO MY DOMAIN IS NONE OTHER THAN AGNAR, THE VANIR...
...WHO HAS SWORN ETERNAL FEALTY TO BALDER!
HE CAN ONLY HAVE COME FROM ASGARD SEEKING HIS LIEGE LORD.
AND SHOULD HE REACH HIM, BALDER WILL LEARN THAT I HAVE NEGLECTED TO TELL HIM OF THE DISAPPEARANCE OF ODIN FROM THE GOLDEN REALM!*
AND THEN I WOULD NOT BE ABLE TO HOLD HIM HERE WITHOUT CHAINS.
WHATEVER HIS MISSION, AGNAR MUST NOT REACH BALDER THE BRAVE!
*THOR 353 FOR THE HISTORIANS AMONGST YOU!

"I MUST ARRANGE A PROPER RECEPTION...

"...FOR THIS YOUNG WARRIOR."

FORGIVE MY HAVING HAD YOU BROUGHT TO NORNKEEP THROUGH THE CRYPTS, MY YOUNG BLADE...

...BUT I HAVE MANY ENEMIES WHO WEAR GUISES FAR FAIRER THAN THINE. WHY HAVE YOU COME TO THE NORN REALM?

YOU MUST NOT DETAIN ME. I HAVE COME WITH A MESSAGE OF GREAT URGENCY FROM **THOR** HIMSELF.

IT IS IM-**PERATIVE** THAT BALDER **RETURN** TO ASGARD AT **ONCE!**

THOR IS ABOUT TO EMBARK ON A MISSION OF THE DEADLIEST NATURE AND HE CRAVES THE NOBLE BALDER'S PRESENCE!

ALAS, YOUNG SIR, I FEAR YOUR SPEECH IS ALL **GIB-BERISH** TO ME!

KAZAPPP!

AND WHEN YOU AWAKEN, GIBBERISH IS **ALL** THAT YOU WILL BE ABLE TO UTTER...

...FOR BALDER MUST NEVER LEARN OF THY MISSION HERE FROM THEE.

33

THOUGH I DO NOT DARE SLAY AGNAR FOR FEAR OF THOR'S WRATH SHOULD HE LEARN OF HIS MESSENGER'S DEATH...

...I WILL PLAY FOR TIME UNTIL THOR HAS LEFT...

...AND THEN WITH A LITTLE PERSUADING, AGNAR SHALL BE MADE TO BELIEVE THAT HE WAS **NEVER** IN NORNKEEP AT ALL!

NOW, PITCH HIM INTO MY DEEPEST DUNGEON.

BUT MARK YOU, KEEP HIM FED AND SECURE TILL I CALL FOR HIM!

*Ah, BALDER, PLEASE FORGIVE MY ABSENCE FROM YOUR SIDE.*

MY LITTLE FRIENDS HAVE KEPT ME AMUSED, KARNILLA.

AND HAVE YOU SET-TLED THE MATTER OF YOUR VISITOR?

HOW... HOW DID YOU KNOW?

A LITTLE BIRD TOLD ME.

HE WAS SIMPLY SOME ITINERANT **TRADES-MAN** SEEKING WORK. I HAVE DISMISSED HIM.

AND I THOUGHT ONLY THE WALLS HAD EARS.

SOME HOURS LATER, IN A BLACK PIT DEEP IN THE BOWELS OF NORNKEEP...

OOH, MY HEAD!

WHAT... WHAT HAS HAPPENED?

I...I CAN'T EVEN RE-MEMBER MY NAME!

AND THEN ... THEN...

THERE WAS A BEAUTIFUL WOMAN AND I HAD SOME-THING IMPORTANT I HAD TO SAY TO SOMEONE!

**SCRAGGUNG!**

KA GRU-GERT?

RYTE! IG THISK MEG RYTE!

34

MY **VOICE!** I CANNOT SPEAK CLEARLY! WHAT HAS HAPPENED TO ME?

WELL, WHAT- EVER MY ENEMIES HAVE IN STORE FOR ME, THEY DON'T MEAN FOR ME TO STARVE TO DEATH!

*U/mmm.* THE WATER TASTES GOOD NO MATTER WHO'S PROVIDING IT. PERHAPS--!

KARGAG!

VETHLY WINROCS!

**KRINNG!**

FILTHY CREATURES!

AND YET, MAY- HAP I HAVE ACTED TOO HASTILY. FOR AM I NOT THE SAME AS THEY?

LOST, ALONE, A MERE SPEECHLESS, BRUTISH THING.

AND I SEEM TO REMEMBER ANOTHER, A GEN- TLE BEING WHO CALLED ANIMALS OF EVERY KIND FRIEND.

"I... I CAN ALMOST SEE HIS FACE BEFORE ME NOW.

"SOMEONE I MUST HAVE KNOWN. RESPECTED. PERHAPS EVEN LOVED."

'TIS AN EXCELLENT LIBATION, KARNILLA.

SURELY THIS MUST BE SOME RARE WINE PROCURED FROM BEYOND THE SHORES OF RINGSFJORD.

WITH THE PASSING OF DAYS, BRAVE BALDER, YOU MAY YET HAVE A CHANCE TO SAMPLE THE MYRIAD DELIGHTS OF MY ENTIRE CELLAR.

AND AS TIME MEANS NOTHING TO SUCH AS WE, WHO KNOWS WHAT RARE AND WONDROUS VINTAGES WE MAY YET ENCOUNTER?

HOW LONG, MY LITTLE ONES? HOW LONG?

IN THIS NEVER CHANGING TWILIGHT, I HAVE LOST ALL TRACK OF DAYS.

BUT AS TIME PASSES, MORE AND MORE OF YOUR KINDRED JOIN US AND SHARE OUR MEAGER RATIONS.

ONLY THUS DO I KNOW THAT THE HOURS INDEED ARE SLOWLY SLIPPING PAST.

AND WITH THEM, I FEEL MY SENSE OF URGENCY SLOWLY SLIPPING AWAY.

IF ONLY I COULD REMEMBER.

YOU KNOW, BALDER, SINCE YOUR ARRIVAL HERE, THE COUNTRYSIDE OF THE NORN-REALM HAS NEVER BEEN SO *GREEN*, SO BEAUTIFUL.

SOMEDAY, I WOULD LIKE TO UNDERSTAND HOW YOU WRAP THE SUNSHINE ABOUT YOU AND WARM THE VERY EARTH.

THE SUN IS IN THE HEART, MILADY, AND YOU HAVE ALWAYS SHEATHED YOURS IN THE FROSTS OF WINTER.

THEN PERHAPS YOU WILL HELP ME TO *MELT* THE SHEATH AND LIE IN THE SUNSHINE, MY LORD.

WHAT SAY YOU, BALDER?

BALDER?

FORGIVE ME, MY LADY.

BUT FROM THIS HIGH PROMONTORY, I FEEL I CAN ALMOST SEE ALL THE WAY HOME TO ASGARD.

...AND ONE DAY, THERE I MUST RETURN.

WHY SHOULD YOU, MY BRAVE WARRIOR.

EVERYTHING YOU WANT IS *HERE*... WITH *ME*.

COME, MY LITTLE FRIENDS, AND EAT.

FOR HERE WE SHARE OUR FOOD AND FATE, HUDDLED IN THE DARKNESS.

AND **YOU** I ENVY MOST OF ALL.

HOW EASILY YOU MAY ESCAPE THIS PLACE AND FLY FREE THOUGH YOU SHUN THE LIGHT.

SQUEEE! SQUEEE!

...AND LEAVE US IN OUR DARKNESS AND DESPAIR.

SQUEEE! SQUEEE!

WHAT IS **THIS?** A BAT IN DAYLIGHT?

WHAT IS IT, LITTLE ONE?

SQUEEE! SQUEEE!

WHAT ERRAND OF URGENCY HAS BROUGHT YOU OUT OF THE STYGIAN DEPTHS TO SEEK THE LIGHT AND BALDER?

BE OFF! BALDER SHALL FOLLOW THEE WITHOUT FAIL...

...THROUGH THE MANY CRYPTS WHERE NE'ER THE SUN HAS SHONE...

...AS SILENTLY AS A SHADOW...

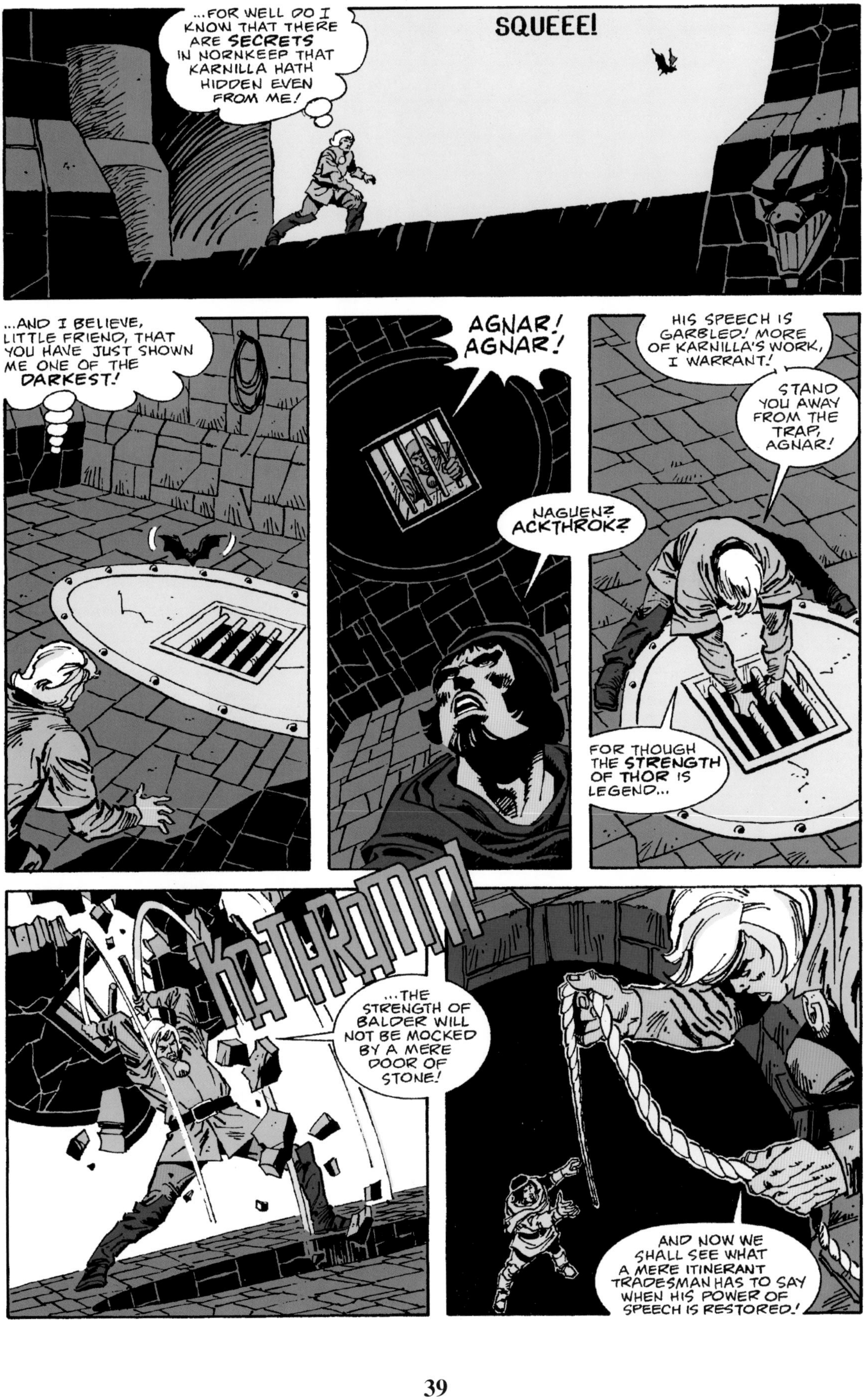
...FOR WELL DO I KNOW THAT THERE ARE SECRETS IN NORNKEEP THAT KARNILLA HATH HIDDEN EVEN FROM ME!
SQUEEE!
...AND I BELIEVE, LITTLE FRIEND, THAT YOU HAVE JUST SHOWN ME ONE OF THE DARKEST!
AGNAR! AGNAR!
NAGUEN? ACKTHROK?
HIS SPEECH IS GARBLED! MORE OF KARNILLA'S WORK, I WARRANT!
STAND YOU AWAY FROM THE TRAP, AGNAR!
FOR THOUGH THE STRENGTH OF THOR IS LEGEND...
KA-THROOM!
...THE STRENGTH OF BALDER WILL NOT BE MOCKED BY A MERE DOOR OF STONE!
AND NOW WE SHALL SEE WHAT A MERE ITINERANT TRADESMAN HAS TO SAY WHEN HIS POWER OF SPEECH IS RESTORED!

THE THRONE ROOM OF KARNILLA...

...FROM WHENCE THE NORN QUEEN GOVERNS HER GREAT REALM AND DISPENSES JUSTICE TO HER SUBJECTS.

THY PLEA IS GRANTED, GNASHNATH. THE TOADS' HEADS SHALL BE THINE.

YOUR MAJESTY IS GRACIOUS TO HER HUMBLE SERVANT.

BUT SHOULD YOU FAIL TO PRODUCE THE WER-GELD...

...THE TOADS SHALL FEAST UPON THINE EYES!

HAVE HIM REMOVED FROM THE COURT, HAAG.

GENERALLY, SUCH PROCEEDINGS RUN SMOOTHLY AND WITHOUT INTERRUPTION...

...BUT TODAY--

I SAID--

STAND ASIDE!!

KRKKRRRUMM!

40

GREETINGS, GRACIOUS QUEEN.

WHAT IS THE MEANING OF THIS INTRUSION, BALDER?

I HAVE COME TO SEEK THE QUEEN'S JUSTICE!

FOR I HAVE FOUND THE ITINERANT TRADESMAN AND I AM SURE THAT YOU CAN HELP HIM.

VERY SURE.

HE SEEMS TO HAVE LOST THE POWER TO SPEAK CLEARLY.

I TOLD HIM THAT I WAS CERTAIN KARNILLA, THE BEAUTIFUL AND GRACIOUS NORN QUEEN, COULD RE-STORE IT.

HAAG, CLEAR THE THRONE ROOM.

NOW!

DID ANOTHER LITTLE BIRD SPEAK TO YOU?

MORE OR LESS.

STAND STILL, AGNAR. IT WILL ONLY STING FOR A MOMENT.

41

Urk!

MY **VOICE**! I CAN **SPEAK** AGAIN! AND I REMEMBER **EVERY-THING**!

MY **LADY**! I...I...

AND HERE, KARNILLA, I THOUGHT THAT YOUR KISSES WERE ONLY FOR ME.

SHE IS A **WONDER**, IS SHE NOT, LAD?

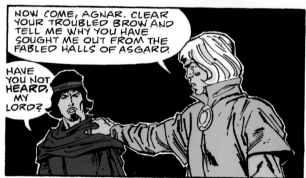

NOW COME, AGNAR. CLEAR YOUR TROUBLED BROW AND TELL ME WHY YOU HAVE SOUGHT ME OUT FROM THE FABLED HALLS OF ASGARD.

HAVE YOU NOT **HEARD**, MY LORD?

ODIN, THE ALL-FATHER HAS PASSED ON. HE AND HIS MORTAL ENEMY, **SUR-TUR**, FELL TOGETHER INTO THE FIERY DEPTHS AND HAVE BEEN SEEN NO MORE.*

THE ALL-FATHER-- **GONE**?!!

AND YOU DID NOT TELL ME, KARNILLA?

TO WHAT **END**? 'TWAS **BEYOND** YOUR POWER TO AID HIM IN THAT FINAL MO-MENT. OR MINE!

BETTER TO STAND IN THE SUN THAN CRY IN THE DARK!

I **DID** TELL THEE, BALDER. EVERY-THING YOU WANT IS **HERE**... WITH ME.

\* THOR 353

MY LORD THOR HAS BID ME COME AND ASK YOU TO RETURN TO THE GOLDEN REALM.

FOR HE PLANS A FORAY INTO **HEL** AND ONLY **BALDER** THE **BRAVE** HATH JOURNEYED THERE AND RETURNED TO TELL THE TALE.

HE NEEDS THE AID ONLY YOU CAN GIVE.

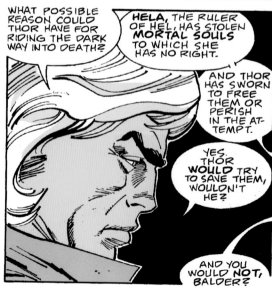

WHAT POSSIBLE REASON COULD THOR HAVE FOR RIDING THE DARK WAY INTO DEATH?

**HELA**, THE RULER OF HEL, HAS STOLEN **MORTAL SOULS** TO WHICH SHE HAS NO RIGHT.

AND THOR HAS SWORN TO FREE THEM OR PERISH IN THE AT-TEMPT.

YES. THOR **WOULD** TRY TO SAVE THEM, WOULDN'T HE?

AND YOU WOULD **NOT**, BALDER?

DO **NOT** DO THIS THING, MY LORD.

WHAT ARE A FEW MORTAL SOULS TO SUCH AS **WE?**

BUT HE IS **RIGHT.** THE REALM OF HELA IS PERILOUS AND AWFUL BEYOND WORDS.

AND **NO** MORTAL WHO HAS NOT EARNED THAT DEATH SHOULD TASTE IT.

THAT JOURNEY WILL BE EASY, LORD BALDER.

BUT FROM THE JOURNEY TO HEL, EVEN **YOU** MAY NOT RETURN!

OF ALL THE LIVING, I ALONE KNOW THE COST OF THE ENTERPRISE THOR IS UNDER- TAKING.

HE MAY **YET** WISH HE HAD DIED BY HIS FATHER'S SIDE!

I WILL RETURN TO ASGARD WITH YOU, AGNAR.

MY LORD, FORGIVE MY IMPERTINENCE, BUT--

THAT IS--

I MEAN, WHY DO YOU--?

STAY WITH THE QUEEN OF THE NORNS, AGNAR?

YOU DO NOT KNOW HER AS I DO.

THERE IS A GREAT DEAL MORE TO KARNILLA THAN JUST THE THWARTED QUEEN.

WHAT WOMAN WHO LOVED A MAN WOULD WANT TO SEE HIM ENTER HEL UNDER ANY CIR- CUMSTANCES?

THE QUEEN WAS SIMPLY PREPARED TO DO MORE ABOUT IT THAN MOST.

I AM DIS- APPOINTED THAT SHE DID NOT TELL ME BEFORE ABOUT ODIN, BUT OF COURSE SHE WAS RIGHT.

I WOULD HAVE RETURNED TO ASGARD LONG SINCE AND LEFT HER BEHIND HAD I KNOWN.

AND IN A SENSE, KARNILLA IMPRISONED **YOU** WITH MY BEST INTERESTS AT HEART.

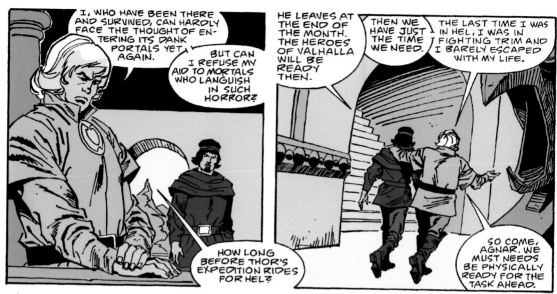

I, WHO HAVE BEEN THERE AND SURVIVED, CAN HARDLY FACE THE THOUGHT OF ENTERING ITS DANK PORTALS YET AGAIN.

BUT CAN I REFUSE MY AID TO MORTALS WHO LANGUISH IN SUCH HORROR?

HOW LONG BEFORE THOR'S EXPEDITION RIDES FOR HEL?

HE LEAVES AT THE END OF THE MONTH. THE HEROES OF VALHALLA WILL BE READY THEN.

THEN WE HAVE JUST THE TIME WE NEED.

THE LAST TIME I WAS IN HEL, I WAS IN FIGHTING TRIM AND I BARELY ESCAPED WITH MY LIFE.

SO COME, AGNAR. WE MUST NEEDS BE PHYSICALLY READY FOR THE TASK AHEAD.

AND FROM THAT TIME FORTH, BALDER SAW NO MORE THE COUNTENANCE OF KARNILLA...

...AS SHE STAYED WITHIN THE CONFINES OF NORN-KEEP AND SPOKE TO NO ONE...

...EXCEPT HAAG.

I SHOULD HAVE HAD AGNAR SLAIN ERE HE CAME WITHIN THE WALLS OF NORN-KEEP.

BUT COULD I HAVE KEPT THE NEWS ABOUT ODIN FROM BALDER FOREVER?

OH, BALDER, WOULD THAT I HAD NEVER SEEN THY BLINDING IMAGE BEFORE MINE EYES!

I AM SO AFRAID FOR THEE!

EVEN NOW, HAAG, I HAVE WITHIN MY CASTLE THE *MEANS* THAT MIGHT SAVE HIM FROM HELA'S ARMS A SECOND TIME.

AND YET, CAN I GIVE UP SO PRICELESS A TREASURE AS THE *SWORD OF FREY*, EVEN TO BALDER?

HE IS NO MEAN WARRIOR BUT ONE OF THE *FINEST* OF ANY REALM!

WOULD HE EVEN NEED SUCH A WEAPON?

KLAAG! KRANGG!

AND STILL, HE AND AGNAR CONTINUE THEIR CEASELESS PRACTICE OUTSIDE IN THE COURTYARD.

WELL STRUCK, MY YOUNG FRIEND. NOW TRY AGAIN. AND THIS TIME, HOLD NOTHING BACK!

BUT BALDER...

ATTACK, AND DO NOT FEAR FOR ME!

SWISSCH!

FOR THIS IS THE *ART* THAT YOU NEED TO MASTER, AGNAR!

THE ART OF BEING *SOMEWHERE ELSE* WHEN THE BLADE TRIES TO BITE!

45

NOW, STRIKE AGAIN! FASTER!

BUT BE-WARE...

...FOR AN ENEMY MAY BE AS FAST ON THE OFFENSE AS ON THE DEFENSE.

THAT WAS WELL DONE.

NOW LET US PLAY AT OTHER GAMES TILL WE HAVE MASTERED THEM ALL...

THACKKT!

SHRANNG!

...TILL WE ARE READY TO WALK INTO HEL AND CHALLENGE DEATH HERSELF TO A DUEL!

...TILL OUR BODIES HAVE BURNED THEMSELVES DOWN TO THEIR ESSENTIAL CORES...

AND AS THE DAYS PASS, THE TWO WARRIORS WORK WITH THE ENERGY OF GODS...

...NEITHER SLEEPING NOR RESTING...

...PAUSING ONLY FOR SUSTENANCE...

KA-CHUNCK!

...CEASELESSLY HONING THEIR SKILLS AND THEIR BODIES.

AND AS THE MONTH WANES, THE TRAINING BECOMES EVEN FIERCER, EVEN HARDER.

COME, AGNAR, CATCH ME IF YOU CAN! WHERE IS THAT YOUNG BLOOD AND FIRE?

THE RISING MOON WATCHES AS THE WARRIORS BELOW SEEM TO FLY ACROSS THE GHOSTLY LANDSCAPE...

...AND THE RISING SUN PEEKS ABOVE THE HORIZON TO FIND THE SAME TWO FIGURES STILL SOARING ACROSS THE PEAKS OF THE NORN REALM...

...NEITHER SLEEPING NOR RESTING...

SLASSH!

326, 327, 328, 329, 330!

...UNTIL AT LAST...

THE HOUR HAS COME, AGNAR!

ONCE MORE, 'TIS TIME TO TAKE UP THE TOYS OF WAR...

...AND RIDE **BOLDLY** OFF INTO THE WAITING ARMS OF THE FATES!

HAIL, SILVER-HOOF! KARNILLA HAS BEEN A GOOD HOSTESS TO YOU, MY STEED.

NEVER HAS YOUR COAT SHONE SO IN THE MORNING SUN.

NEVER HAVE YOU LOOKED SO **BEAUTIFUL.**

SO EVEN NOW, BALDER CAN SPARE A THOUGHT FOR THE QUEEN OF THIS LAND AS ONLY A **STABLE HAND...**

...FIT TO CURRY THE HORSES BUT **NOT** FIT TO SPEAK WITH THE HEROES THAT RIDE THEM.

YOU WOULD DO BETTER TO LOOK TO ME FOR HELP THAN BE OFF SO HURRIEDLY TO THE KINGDOM OF DEATH.

I AM SORRY, MY QUEEN, THAT YOU VIEW OUR LEAVE-TAKING SO HARSHLY...

...BUT YOU WOULD LOVE ME **LESS** IF I DID NOT RIDE WITH THOR TO A SPLENDID DOOM.

48

AND I SHALL LOVE YOU **NOT AT ALL** WHEN YOU **FAIL** TO RETURN.

HOW DIFFERENT, PRAY TELL, WOULD **THAT** BE FROM THE **PAST** WEEK?

YOU SPEAK NASTY TO GREAT QUEEN!

DEATH TO QUEEN'S ENEMIES!!

BALDER!

FEAR NOT.

THE DEMON DOES NOT LIVE WHO COULD TOUCH BALDER UNLESS HE WILLED IT.

FAUGGH-- SPUTTT!

COME, MY FRIEND. LET ME RETURN YOUR SPEAR AND YOUR GOOD HUMOR.

HOW **DARE** YOU ATTACK WITHOUT ORDERS, DOG!

MUST I AGAIN TEACH YOU YOUR **PLACE**?

NO!

SPARE HIM, KARNILLA, FOR MY SAKE. HE BUT ATTACKED OUT OF LOVE FOR HIS MISTRESS.

WHAT DOES A WARRIOR NEED WHO CAN SO EASILY DEFEAT ONE OF MY PICKED GUARDS?

HOW ABOUT YOUR **BLESSING** TO TAKE WITH US INTO THE DARKEST REALMS OF DEATH?

NO?

BUT TELL ME, DID YOU NOT SPEAK OF **HELP** A MOMENT AGO?

KARNILLA HAS **NOTHING** THAT WOULD AID SUCH A MIGHTY FIGHTER!

THEN YOU SHALL HAVE **MINE!**

MAY THY SHEATH OF ICE **MELT** BEFORE THE SUN RETURNS!

FARE YOU WELL, MY QUEEN.

DOG, THAT YOU WOULD HAVE **HARMED** MY **BALDER!!**

NOW, BEGONE, ALL OF YOU!

SZZLAAPP!!

...AND SLOWLY...

...NIGHT COMES TO THE ANCIENT REALM.

MAY THE NORNS GUIDE YOU, SWEET WARRIOR, AND BRING YOU BACK SAFELY TO ME.

DON'T MISS **BALDER'S RIDE** INTO HEL WITH **THOR** AND THE **HEROES OF VALHALLA** IN THOR **360!** AND IN **TWO** MONTHS, WE'LL RETURN TO KARNILLA'S REALM TO FIND IT **RAVAGED** AND **DESOLATE** BECAUSE OF-- BUT THAT WOULD BE TELLING!

BE HERE NEXT ISSUE FOR:

# Balder the Betrayed!

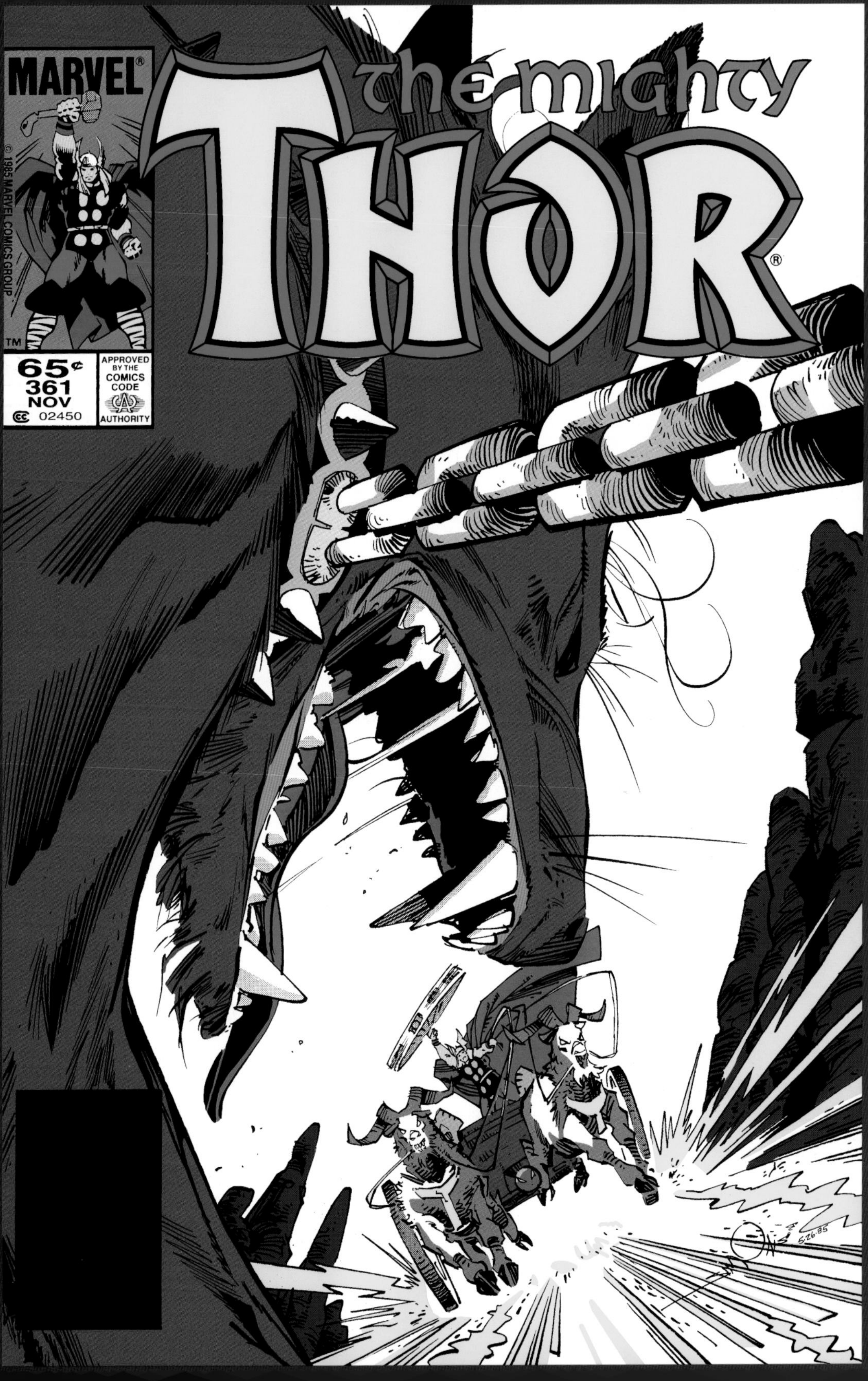
MARVEL®
THE MIGHTY
THOR®
© 1985 MARVEL COMICS GROUP
TM
65¢
361
NOV
02450
APPROVED BY THE COMICS CODE AUTHORITY
5.26.85

"GARM BAYS LOUDLY BEFORE GNIPA CAVE; HIS CHAIN WILL BREAK AND HE WILL RUN FREE."*

IN THE **SHADOW** OF THE **BEAST** STANDS THE ENTRANCE TO **HEL**...

...AND 'TIS THROUGH THAT DOLEFUL GATEWAY **THOR** MUST RIDE WITH HIS COMPANIONS!

HO, GARM! FIERCEST OF HOUNDS! THE SON OF ODIN GREETS THEE!

HAIL, MIGHTY THOR. HELA, MY MISTRESS, WARNED ME THAT YOU MIGHT WISH TO USE THE HELWAY.

WOULD YOU SEEK THE KINGDOM OF THE DEAD AS A LIVING MAN?

BEWARE THOSE WHO ENTER HERE DO NOT COME OUT AGAIN.

# THE QUICK AND THE DEAD!

*THE SIBYL'S PROPHECY

**WALTER SIMONSON**
ART & STORY

**JOHN WORKMAN, JR.**
LETTERING

**"MAX" SCHEELE**
COLORS

**RALPH MACCHIO**
EDITING

**JIM SHOOTER**
ED. IN CHIEF

THE BLOOD OF THOR SHALL NOT EASILY STAIN YOUR BREAST, GARM...

...LIKE THE BLOOD OF SO MANY OTHERS WHO SOUGHT TO LEAVE HELA'S REALM.

WITH YOUR PERMISSION, WE WOULD ENTER HER DOMAIN.

I SHALL MAKE THE ARRANGEMENTS FOR OUR DEPARTURE.

I AM CALLED THE DOOM OF TYR, MIGHTY THOR. PERHAPS SOMEDAY, I SHALL BE CALLED THE DOOM OF THOR AS WELL.

YOU AND YOUR COMPANIONS MAY ENTER FREELY AND OF YOUR OWN WILL.

HAROKIN, ORDER THE WARRIORS AND FOLLOW ME INTO THE CAVE OF DARKNESS.

EXECUTIONER, BRING UP THE REAR AND GUARD IT WELL.

FAREWELL, YOU EINHERJAR, BOLD HEROES OF VALHALLA.

PRAY THAT GARM NEVER AGAIN SEES THY FACES IN THE LIGHT.

BUT THE ONLY SOUND THAT ECHOES IN THE VALLEY OF DEATH IS THE TINKLING OF THE HARNESSES AND THE CLATTER OF THE ARMOR...

...UNTIL AT LAST, THE EXECUTIONER ENTERS THE DARKNESS AND THE SILENCE OF THE VALLEY IS AGAIN UNBROKEN.

THE ROAD TO HEL, MIGHTY THOR, MAY BE PAVED WITH GOOD INTENTIONS...

...BUT THE DARKNESS OF THE HELWAY IS HARDLY A MATCH FOR THE BLACKNESS IN MY HEART.

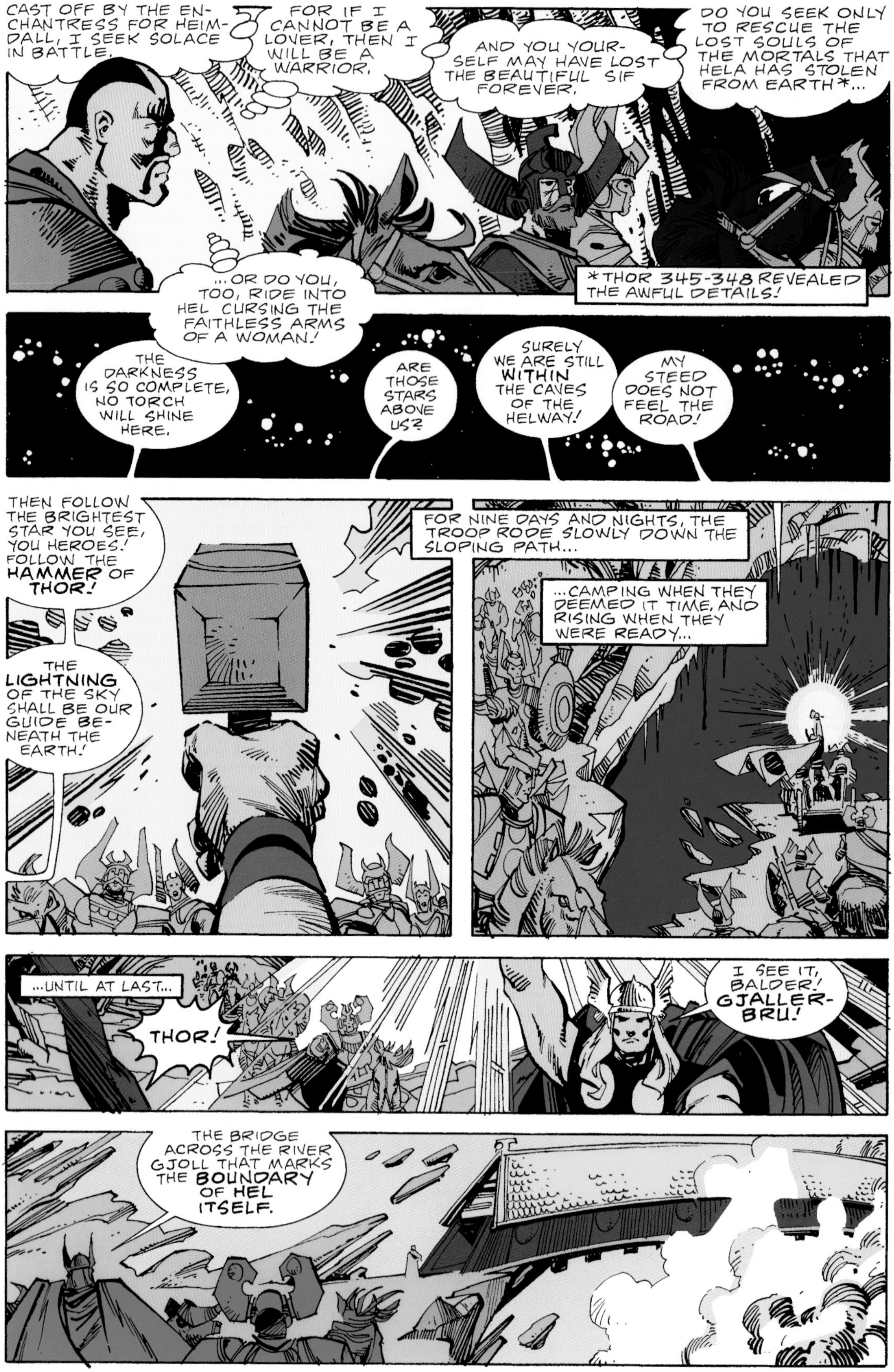
CAST OFF BY THE ENCHANTRESS FOR HEIMDALL, I SEEK SOLACE IN BATTLE.
FOR IF I CANNOT BE A LOVER, THEN I WILL BE A WARRIOR.
AND YOU YOURSELF MAY HAVE LOST THE BEAUTIFUL SIF FOREVER.
DO YOU SEEK ONLY TO RESCUE THE LOST SOULS OF THE MORTALS THAT HELA HAS STOLEN FROM EARTH*...
...OR DO YOU, TOO, RIDE INTO HEL CURSING THE FAITHLESS ARMS OF A WOMAN!
*THOR 345-348 REVEALED THE AWFUL DETAILS!
THE DARKNESS IS SO COMPLETE, NO TORCH WILL SHINE HERE.
ARE THOSE STARS ABOVE US?
SURELY WE ARE STILL WITHIN THE CAVES OF THE HELWAY!
MY STEED DOES NOT FEEL THE ROAD!
THEN FOLLOW THE BRIGHTEST STAR YOU SEE, YOU HEROES! FOLLOW THE HAMMER OF THOR!
THE LIGHTNING OF THE SKY SHALL BE OUR GUIDE BENEATH THE EARTH!
FOR NINE DAYS AND NIGHTS, THE TROOP RODE SLOWLY DOWN THE SLOPING PATH...
...CAMPING WHEN THEY DEEMED IT TIME, AND RISING WHEN THEY WERE READY...
...UNTIL AT LAST...
THOR!
I SEE IT, BALDER! GJALLERBRU!
THE BRIDGE ACROSS THE RIVER GJOLL THAT MARKS THE BOUNDARY OF HEL ITSELF.

AND THERE BEFORE THE BRIDGE IS ITS GUARDIAN, MODGUD, WHOSE SILENCE IS THAT OF THE GRAVE MOUND!

HAIL, MODGUD. THE SON OF ODIN AND HIS COMPANIONS GREET THEE.

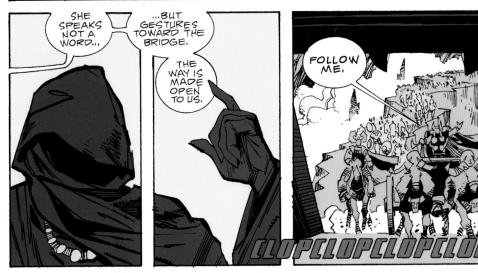

SHE SPEAKS NOT A WORD...

...BUT GESTURES TOWARD THE BRIDGE.

THE WAY IS MADE OPEN TO US.

FOLLOW ME,

CLOPCLOPCLOPCLOPCLOPCL

I HAVE PASSED THE WORD TO THE EINHERJAR TO KEEP THEIR WEAPONS AT THE READY...

...FOR WE ARE NEARLY THERE AND HELA DOUBTLESS AWAITS US.

I SEE THE LIGHT BEYOND THE BRIDGE...

...BUT I DO NOT RECOGNIZE THE COUNTRY!!

THE SWEET MELODIES OF SONG BIRDS FILL THE AIR, THE SWEET BREEZES CARESS THE CHEEKS...

...AND THE LANDSCAPE BEFORE THEM IS SUFFUSED WITH A WONDERFUL BRILLIANCE.

BALDER! WHERE ARE WE?

SURELY THIS LAND OF ENCHANTMENT CANNOT BE HEL.

BUT EVEN AS THE COMPANY ADVANCES FUR-
THER INTO THE RADIANT VISION BEFORE
THEM...

I DO NOT LIKE THIS PLACE.

THE WHOLE WORLD SINGS OF PEACE AND HARMONY!

ARGH! THIS IS NO PLACE FOR A FIGHTING MAN!

MAYBE I SHOULD NOT HAVE COME HERE.

BUT THEN, SKURGE, YOU WOULD NOT HAVE FOUND ME AGAIN.

HUH?

ENCHANTRESS! WHAT ARE YOU DO-ING IN THIS PLACE?

HUSH, SKURGE, AND HOLD ME! KISS ME AS THOUGH YOU'LL NEVER LET ME GO!

AND A LONG MOMENT LATER...

BUT AMORA! IS THIS NOT...?

YES, SKURGE, IT IS THE LAND OF THE DEAD, AND I BELONG HERE NOW.

FOR JEALOUS HEIMDALL SLEW ME WHEN HE FOUND THAT I WOULD REMAIN TRUE TO YOU.

WHAT?!! BY THE GODS, HE SHALL PAY FOR THIS.

NO, SKURGE! LEAVE HIM BE, FOR I DO NOT WISH EVER TO BE PARTED FROM YOU AGAIN.

LET THE ASGARDIANS GO. STAY WITH ME HERE AND NEVER LEAVE ME.

BUT THOR...?

IS THE GOD OF THUNDER AND NEEDS NO HELP FROM ANY-ONE.

BUT I... I NEED YOU NOW MORE THAN EVER.

56

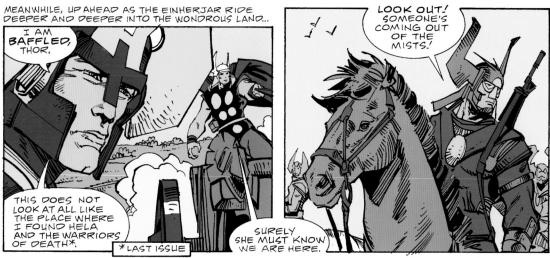

MEANWHILE, UP AHEAD AS THE EINHERJAR RIDE DEEPER AND DEEPER INTO THE WONDROUS LAND...

I AM **BAFFLED,** THOR.

THIS DOES NOT LOOK AT ALL LIKE THE PLACE WHERE I FOUND HELA AND THE WARRIORS OF DEATH*.

*LAST ISSUE

SURELY SHE MUST KNOW WE ARE HERE.

LOOK OUT! SOMEONE'S COMING OUT OF THE MISTS!

I CAN'T QUITE SEE THEM CLEARLY!

READY YOUR WEAPONS!

WAIT! HOLD YOUR FIRE!

IT'S MY **SON** WHO **DIED** IN THE **BURN-ING** OF NJAL!

AND THERE'S MY **WIFE!**

THIS IS **TRULY** THE REALM OF THE DEAD!

OUR LOVERS AND LOVED ONES HAVE COME TO GREET US!

AND IN THE NEXT INSTANT...

...FAMILIES LONG SUNDERED BY DEATH ARE JOINED TOGETHER AMID GREAT REJOICING FOR THE FIRST TIME SINCE THEIR PARTING.

ELSEWHERE, IN ASGARD, IN THE CITY OF THE GODS...

THE RE-BUILDING OF THE GOLDEN REALM CONTINUES APACE, FRIGGA.

SOMEDAY, THE DESTRUCTION WROUGHT BY SURTUR WILL BE ONLY A MEMORY, SIF.

HOW CAN YOU OF ALL PEOPLE SAY THAT TIME WILL HEAL OUR WOUNDS, YOU WHO HAVE LOST ODIN?

HIS LOSS, SIF, WAS WORTH THE PRICE.

FOR THE NINE WORLDS STILL ENDURE AND THAT WAS EVER ODIN'S FIRST CONCERN.

THE ORDER WILL CONTINUE.

WHEN THOR RETURNS, WE WILL HOLD THE ALTHING AND A NEW RULER WILL BE CHOSEN IN ASGARD.

I HAVE ONLY MEMORIES TO CONSOLE ME AND THE NIGHTS WILL BE LONG.

YET I WOULD NOT BELITTLE ODIN'S SACRIFICE BY WISHING HIM BACK.

I WAS HIS WIFE, NOW I AM HIS WIDOW, I AM CONTENT.

FORGIVE MY RASH WORDS, FRIGGA.

SHOULD I BE BITTER?

WE ARE A PROUD RACE AND THOR AND I PERHAPS MOST OF ALL...

WHO WOULD HAVE THOUGHT THAT SUCH PRIDE COULD BE HUMBLED BY A SINGLE BLOW*?

I RETURNED TO ASGARD, FRIGGA, FULL OF HOPE, FULL OF LIFE.

AND ALL SEEMS TURNED TO ASHES BEHIND ME.

I LONG TO BE GONE.

WHEN THE ALTHING IS DONE AND THE NEW RULER CROWNED, I SHALL LEAVE THE GOLDEN REALM AGAIN, PERHAPS FOREVER.

*THOR 359 HAS THE UNBELIEVABLE DETAILS.

OUR WARRIORS ARE DISPERSING WITH THEIR LONG LOST FAMILIES, THOR.

LOOK! THOUGH THE LANDSCAPE LIES CLEARLY BEFORE US, THE EINHERJAR ARE VANISHING AS IF THEY WERE WALKING INTO A MIST.

CALL THEM BACK UNTIL WE CAN DECIDE OUR BEST COURSE.

WE MUST FIND HELA.

DO YOU NOT THINK, DEAR BALDER, THAT HELA CAN WAIT?

AFTER ALL, IT WAS SHE WHO HAS PERMITTED US TO BE REUNITED WITH OUR LOVED ONES.

WHO--?

BALDER, MY BELOVED, HAVE YOU SO SOON FORGOTTEN ME? I AM SHE WHO GAVE HER LIFE FOR YOURS.

NANNA!!

TO SEE YOU AGAIN IS TO SEE THE SUN SHINING IN HEL AS IT HAS NOT DONE SINCE THE BEGINNING OF TIME.

TOUCH ME. AM I NOT REAL? HOW I HAVE AWAITED THIS MOMENT.

COME, WALK WITH ME A LITTLE.

I SHALL NOT KEEP THEE LONG FROM THY DUTY.

THEY, TOO, BEGIN TO VANISH INTO THE MIST.

BALDER!

LET THEM GO, MIGHTY THOR. FOR THEIR HEARTS HAVE MUCH TO SAY TO ONE ANOTHER...

...AS HAVE OURS.

SIF! SURELY YOU ARE NOT--!

NAY, THOR, I AM **NOT DEAD.**

BUT I COULD NOT LET MATTERS REST BETWEEN US AS THEY WERE AND RODE AFTER YOU INTO THE LOWER DEPTHS.

I HAVE COME TO ASK YOUR **FORGIVENESS** FOR TREATING YOU SO BADLY...

...AND WHAT BETTER PLACE TO FIND YOU THAN IN THIS HAPPY LAND OF RECONCILIATION AND LOVE?

I AM READY TO DO THY EVERY BIDDING.

INDEED, MILADY. I THINK YOU MAY BE **JUST** THE ONE I HAVE BEEN LOOKING FOR.

FOR THOUGH THE LADY SIF AND I HAVE HAD OUR DIFFERENCES...

...THESE WORDS ARE NOT THOSE OF THE PROUD SHIELD MAIDEN OF ASGARD.

THOR?

SHE WOULD **NEVER** LOVE ME IN SUCH A FASHION...

...NOR WOULD I WISH HER TO.

**SNAP!**

THOR! WHAT ARE YOU **DOING?!**

MERELY TAKING A PRECAUTION, MY LADY!

I THOUGHT TO MAKE AN **OFFERING** TO THE LADY OF THE HARVEST...

**FZZIKKKT!**

60

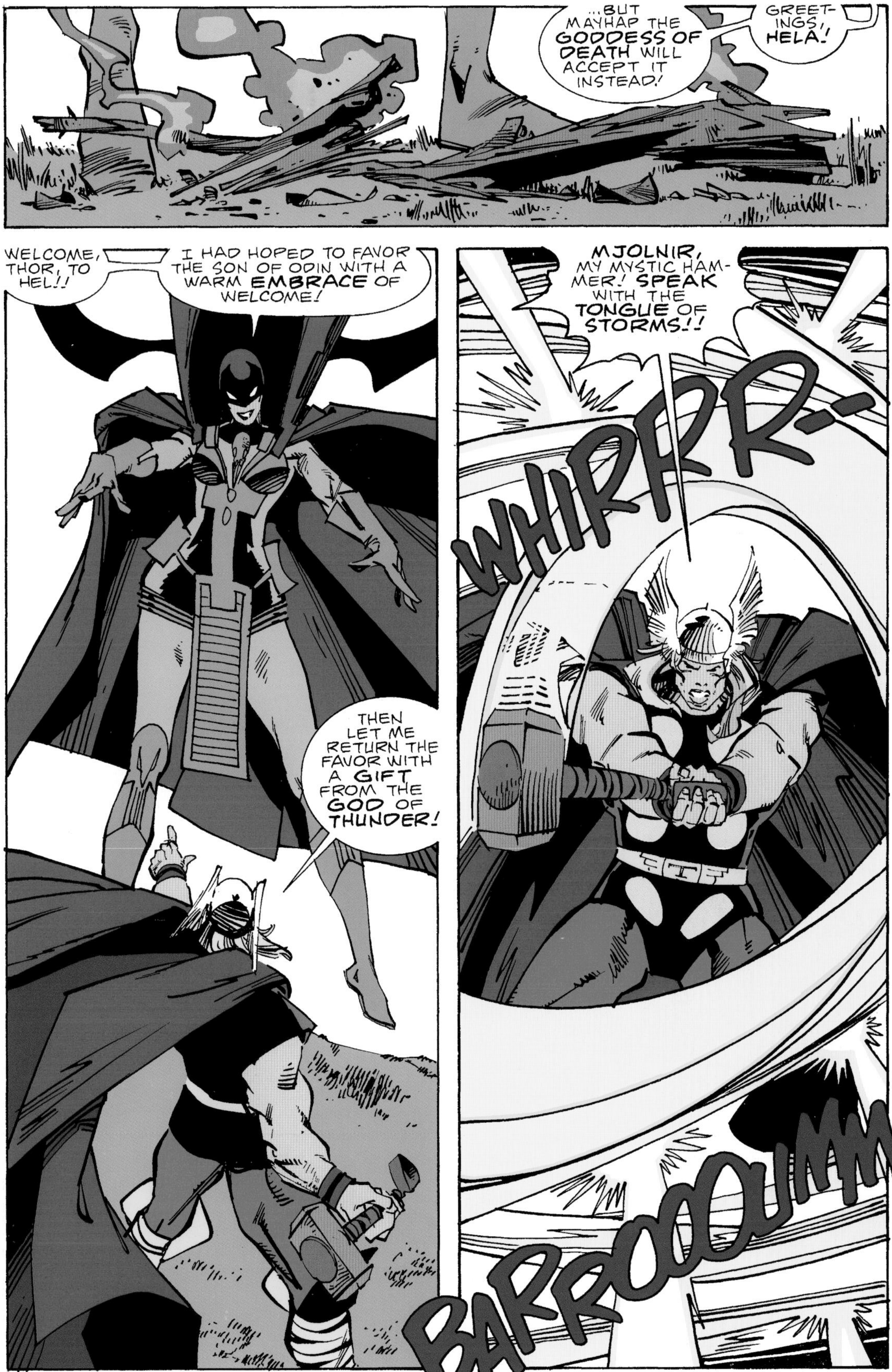
...BUT MAYHAP THE GODDESS OF DEATH WILL ACCEPT IT INSTEAD!
GREET- INGS, HELA!
WELCOME, THOR, TO HEL!!
I HAD HOPED TO FAVOR THE SON OF ODIN WITH A WARM EMBRACE OF WELCOME!
THEN LET ME RETURN THE FAVOR WITH A GIFT FROM THE GOD OF THUNDER!
MJOLNIR, MY MYSTIC HAM- MER! SPEAK WITH THE TONGUE OF STORMS!!
WHIRRR--
BARROOOMM!

...AND REVEAL TO ALL THE FACE OF THE LAND THROUGH WHICH WE WALK!

FOR THESE ARE TRULY THE DEPTHS OF HEL!

BALDER, BEWARE! THE CLIFFS OF DEATH LIE AT THY VERY FEET!

ALREADY SOME OF OUR COMRADES HAVE FALLEN TO THEIR DOOM!

WHAT?

ONE MORE STEP, BALDER MY LOVE! JUST ONE MORE STEP AND YOU WILL JOIN ME FOREVER!

NANNA!!

OH!

NO ONE MAY TOUCH BALDER IF HE DOES NOT WISH IT!

COME, LITTLE ONES!

GATHER 'ROUND THAT I MAY SEE THY SMILING FACES ONCE AGAIN!

TOO LONG HAVE WE TARRIED ON MIDGARD.

WELL MET, MY POP-PETS!

HI, FANDRAL!

WHERE ARE OUR PRESENTS?

WHY, WHAT IS THIS?

LOOK WHAT I HAVE FOUND WITHIN MY GLOVE, GUDRUN.

LET US SEE WHAT ELSE MAY LIE IN MY GLOVES ...OR BENEATH MY TUNIC!

FLOSI! NO TICK-LING NOW!

WELL MET, HILDY.

I HAVE BROUGHT YOU A PRESENT FROM A CHILD OF MIDGARD.

IT WILL SUIT YOU, I THINK.

OH, HOGUN.

*SEE POWER PACK 15 FOR DETAILS!

**67**

AT LAST I AM FREE OF THOR'S GRIP OF IRON!

IF SHE ATTAINS THE AIR AGAIN, I AM **LOST!**

THUS, SHE SHALL NOT GAIN IT!

THRAAMM

YOU WERE **RIGHT**, THOR. THERE IS **NO** WARRIOR IN ALL OF HEL WHO COULD BEST YOU!

NEVER HAS DEATH BEEN SO NEAR DEFEAT!

BUT HELA IS NO ORDINARY WARRIOR...

...AND MINE ARE NOT A WARRIOR'S WEAPONS!

YOU FORCE ME TO DO WHAT EVEN **I** CANNOT UNDO!

RAISE YOUR EYES, THOR...

...AND SEE THE **HAND OF GLORY!**

SLAAASSHH!

GAGGGH!

I HAD HOPED TO WIN YOU UNMARRED, THOR...

...BUT YOU ARE TOO FIERCE A FIGHTER EVEN FOR HELA!

MY FACE!!

NOW FEEL THE UNBREAKABLE GRIP OF OLD AGE...

...AND DESPAIR!

FSSSSSSSTTHU!!

AS YOU SAID, THOR, THE NEXT ONE WHO STOOD WOULD BE THE VICTOR.

MY FACE! THE AGONY IS BEYOND BELIEF!

I FEEL AS THOUGH MY **JAW** HAS BEEN TORN AWAY...

...AND MY LIMBS TREMBLE WITH THE AGUE OF TIME!

IN MOMENTS, I SHALL CRUMBLE TO DUST!

I AM PLEASED, THOR. NO WHIMPERING FOR MERCY, NO BEGGING FOR PITY.

I MAY NOT HAVE THE **FATHER**, BUT THE **SON** IS MINE!

KISS THE HEM OF MY CAPE, THOR...

...AND I MAY GRANT YOU THE PRIVILEGE OF BEING MY SERVANT...

...THE SLAVE OF MY EVERY WHIM, BODY AND SOUL.

**NEVER!**

FOR I HAVE BEEN THE SLAVE OF **ANOTHER** AND HURT THE ONE I LOVE BITTERLY!

IN THE NAME OF MY FATHER, **NEVER** AGAIN SHALL THOR BE SLAVE TO ANY CREATURE!

SOONER WOULD I DIE A THOUSAND DEATHS!

**ARRGHH!**

YOU WRETCH!

MY **CLOAK!** GIVE ME BACK MY **CLOAK!**

HELA! HER...HER FORM IS SHIFTING!

HALF HER BODY IS DYING! IT IS DEAD ALREADY!

70

THOR... (GASP)! ...THOR...

MY OWN BODY FALTERS AS IT AGES FASTER AND FASTER. I HAVE ALMOST NO TIME LEFT.

BUT PERHAPS I HAVE ENOUGH.

STAY WHERE YOU ARE, HELA.

thor!

FOR NOW...I UNDERSTAND.

WITHOUT IT, YOU ARE TRAPPED HERE LIKE YOUR SUBJECTS!

IRONIC, IS IT NOT...

...THAT I WHO HAVE DESTROYED MOUNTAINS AND LEVELED GREAT CITIES...

YOU ARE THE RULER HERE BUT ALSO THE SERVANT. AND THIS CLOAK IS YOUR KEY.

...CAN BARELY MUSTER THE STRENGTH TO TEAR A SCRAP OF CLOTH!

BUT I WILL DESTROY IT, HELA, IF YOU DO NOT ABIDE BY OUR BARGAIN.

IS THE MATCH OVER?

WELL, DEATH?

RIPPPPP

I DO NOT HEAR YOUR ANSWER.

STOP!

THE MATCH IS YOURS.

THE BARGAIN STANDS.

WELL SAID. ALREADY, I FEEL MY YOUTH RE-TURNING.

HAVE YOUR SERVANTS PREPARE THE MORTAL SOULS FOR THEIR DE-PARTURE FROM THIS DESOLATE REALM.

BALDER, SEE TO IT.

AT ONCE, THOR.

BUT THOUGH WE HAVE SAVED THE MORTALS, I AM HEART-SICK.

I HAVE **NOT** FOUND MY FATHER.

THOR?

HIS FACE!! HELA HAS DESTROYED IT!

WHAT DO YOU WANT, NANNA? YOU HAVE BETRAYED THE GOD WHO ONCE LOVED YOU.

WE... WE ARE ALL HELA'S SLAVES, THOR, AND MUST DO HER BID-DING.

I WOULD NOT HAVE SHOWN MY-SELF TO BALDER HAD SHE NOT COMMAND-ED IT.

FOR WELL I KNOW THAT IF HE THOUGHT I STILL LOVED HIM...

...HE WOULD NOT LEAVE ME HERE BUT DIE THE REAL DEATH TO REMAIN BE-SIDE ME.

I COULD NOT FORGIVE MY-SELF WERE I TO ROB THE WORLD OF HIS LIGHT.

AND I CANNOT LEAVE HERE.

NOW, HE THINKS ME SOMETHING COR-RUPTED BEYOND RE-DEMPTION AND WILL RETURN TO HIS PLACE IN THE SUN.

THAT THOUGHT, AND THE KNOWLEDGE THAT YOU KNOW THE TRUTH, WILL SUSTAIN ME HERE.

NANNA!

LEAVE ME, THOR, WHILE I AM STILL RESOLVED. BUT PROMISE ME NEVER TO TELL ANOTHER WHAT I HAVE TOLD YOU.

PROMISE.

YOU HAVE MY WORD.

SO THIS IS HOW IT ENDS.

SIF, IF WE LIVE TO SEE AGAIN THE WALLS OF ASGARD, I WILL BEG THY FORGIVENESS...

FOR IN MY PRIDE, I WOULD HAVE TAKEN IT ONLY ON MY OWN TERMS.

BUT NOW, WHETHER YOU WILL FORGIVE ME OR NOT...

72

I WILL WALK WITH A LIGHTER HEART KNOWING THAT A LOVE LIKE THIS CAN EXIST BEYOND DEATH.

PERHAPS IN TIME, I, TOO, MIGHT BE WORTHY OF SUCH A PERFECT LOVE.

THOR, DID YOU HEAR ME?

WE ARE READY TO DEPART.

I WILL BIND THEM IN THE REMNANTS OF MY CAPE FOR NOW.

LEAD ON, BRAVE BALDER.

BY THE EYE OF ODIN!! THOR'S FACE!!

WHAT... OF YOUR WOUNDS?

THEY ARE AS NOTHING COMPARED TO THOSE THAT OTHERS MUST BEAR.

LET THE BARGAIN BE COMPLETE.

THE CLOAK IS HELA'S ONCE MORE.

AND THIS VICTORY IS THINE, THOR.

BUT THINK NOT TO TELL THE TALE OF YOUR TRIUMPH IN THE MEAD HALLS OF THE GOLDEN REALM...

...FOR THE ROAD FROM HEL IS MORE DANGEROUS THAN YOU COULD KNOW...

...AND IN THE END...

...HELA SHALL HOLD EVERYTHING IN HER HANDS!

NEXT: DAY OF WRATH!

IN WHICH SOME OF THOSE WHO RODE TO HEL DO NOT RIDE OUT AGAIN!

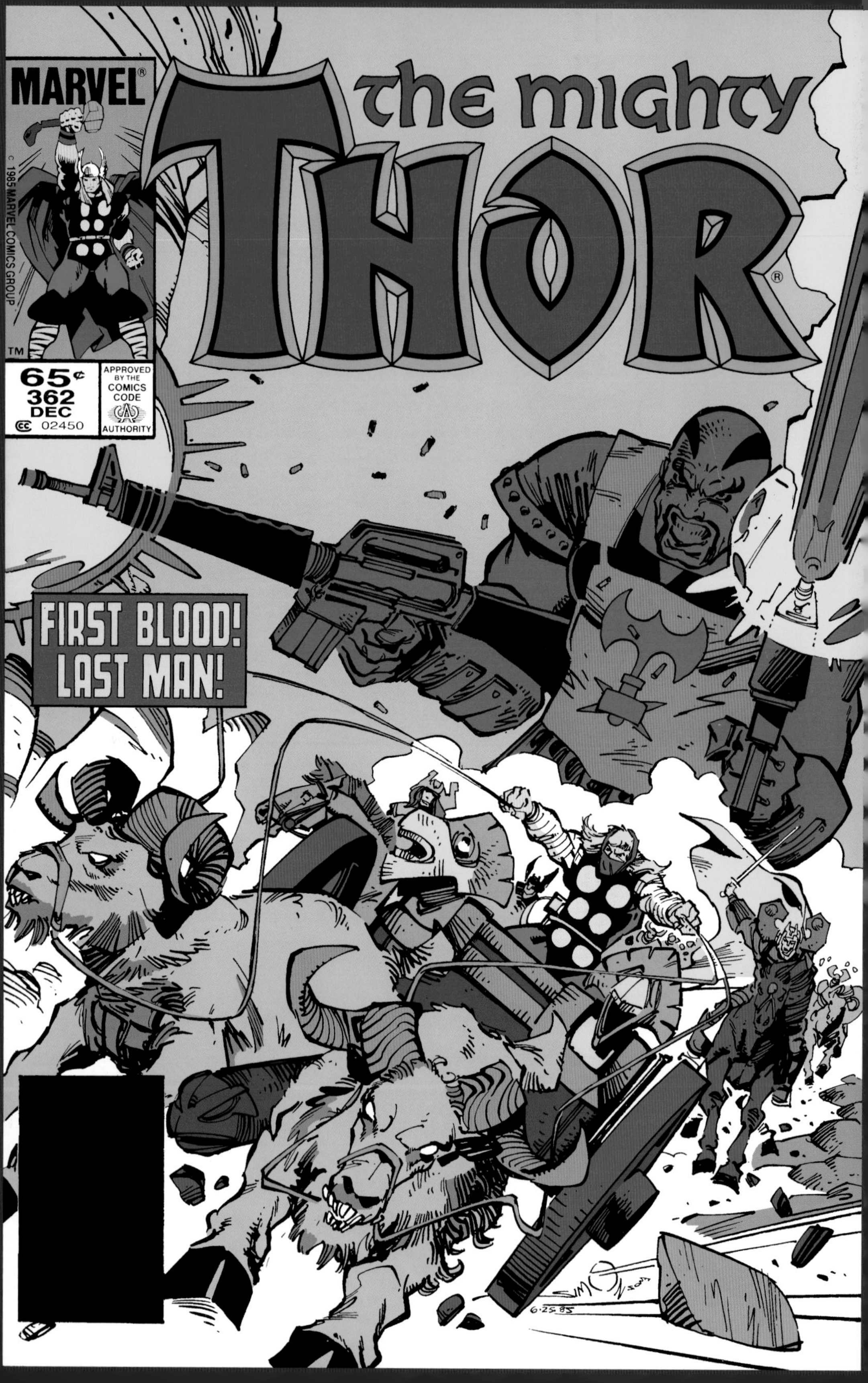
MARVEL®
the mighty
THOR®
© 1985 MARVEL COMICS GROUP
TM
65¢
362
DEC
02450
APPROVED BY THE COMICS CODE AUTHORITY
FIRST BLOOD! LAST MAN!

STAN LEE PRESENTS: the MIGHTY THOR

# LIKE A BAT OUT OF HEL!

ONE OF THE NINE WORLDS IS THE DESOLATE REALM OF HEL INHABITED BY THE SHADES OF THE DEAD.

BUT TODAY, THE HEROES OF VALHALLA, THE EINHERJAR, RIDE THEIR SHINING HORSES THROUGH THAT ANCIENT KINGDOM...

...AND THE NOISE OF THE PASSING ARMY ECHOES LOUDLY IN THE SILENT HALLS OF DEATH.

LOOK, THOR. WHAT GREAT SHIP SITS YONDER BY THE COLD SEA?

NAGLFAR SHE IS CALLED, HAROKIN, AND SHE HAS BEEN A-BUILDING SINCE THE DAWN OF TIME.

'TIS SAID TO BE MADE OF THE FINGERNAILS OF DEAD MEN...

...AND WHEN SHE IS FINISHED, THE DEAD WILL SAIL HER TO ASGARD TO DESTROY THE GODS.

WALTER SIMONSON--STORY & ART. JOHN WORKMAN, JR.--LETTERING. MAX SCHEELE--COLORS. RALPH MACCHIO--EDITING. JIM SHOOTER--EDITOR IN CHIEF.

BUT LONG MAY IT BE TILL **THAT** DAY IS COME.

AND NOW THAT WE HAVE RECOVERED THE SOULS HELA STOLE FROM THE MORTAL REALM *...

...LET US HOPE THAT WE NEVER AGAIN BEHOLD NAFLGAR TILL THE LAST THREAD OF THE FATES IS BROKEN.

*DETAILS LAST ISSUE

OUR TASK WILL BE FINISHED, BALDER, WHEN THESE POOR SPIRITS HAVE BEEN RETURNED TO EARTH.

CAN YOU GUIDE US OUT OF THIS PLACE?

I HAVE TROD THE HELWAY BEFORE. NOT FAR AHEAD IS THE BRIDGE, GJALLERBRU, THAT MARKS THE ENDING OF THE REALM.

...THOUGH THE WOUNDS YOU SUFFERED IN YOUR DUEL WITH THE MISTRESS OF DEATH BELIE THE WORD "EASILY."

BUT I MISTRUST HELA. SURELY SHE WILL NOT LET US RIDE SO EASILY FROM HER DOORS...

HOW IS YOUR FACE?

THE HURT SEEMS AS FRESH AS WHEN HELA STRUCK ME WITH HER HAND OF GLORY.

BUT THE SON OF ODIN DOES NOT TAKE HIS GUARDIANSHIP OF MIDGARD* LIGHTLY, BALDER.

*EARTH

MAYHAP IN TIME, THE AGONY WILL HEAL.

AND MAYHAP, THOR, YOU WILL **ALWAYS** BEAR THE AGONY TO REMIND YOU OF YOUR RASHNESS WHEN YOU INVADED HELA'S KINGDOM.

IF WE HAVE TRULY SAVED THESE MORTALS FROM THEIR UNJUST DOOM IN HEL, I THINK IT WILL HAVE BEEN WORTH THE COST.

76

RATHER, IT WILL REMIND ME THAT EVEN **YOU** MAY NOT UPSET THE BALANCE OF LIFE AND DEATH, HELA.

OR HAVE YOU FORGOTTEN THE ONE WHO ABANDONED YOU UPON YOUR ARRIVAL IN HEL...

...THE EXECUTIONER!

**WHAT?!**

...THOUGH **YOU** RULE THIS REALM FOREVER.

HAVE YOU COME TO DISPUTE OUR DEPARTURE?

ON THE CONTRARY. I MERELY THOUGHT YOU SHOULD TAKE **ALL** YOUR FELLOWS WITH YOU WHEN YOU LEAVE.

SO, SKURGE, I SEE NOW WHY YOU LEFT US BEHIND.

THE ENCHANTRESS HAS EVER COMMANDED YOUR HEART BEFORE ALL OTHER LOYALTIES.

AND DOES STILL, THOR.

I WILL STAND BESIDE HER HERE AGAINST ANY THAT TRY TO STOP ME.

BUT WHO STANDS BESIDE **YOU**, SKURGE?

IN THIS PLACE, ALL THINGS ARE HELA'S, AND **NOTHING** IS WHAT IT SEEMS.

DO NOT LISTEN TO THEM, BELOVED. THEY WOULD TEAR US APART AS THEY HAVE ALWAYS DONE.

YET BALDER SPOKE AND THE BRIGHT ONE **NEVER** LIES!

FORGIVE ME, MY LOVE, BUT I MUST SEE FOR MYSELF.

THE EXECUTIONER'S AXE CAN CUT THROUGH **ANY** DISGUISE TO REVEAL THE TRUE BEING BENEATH!

SKURGE! **NO!**

77

OH, DARLING, WHAT HAVE YOU **DONE**?

DID I NOT WARN YOU TO BE CAREFUL?

NOW THEY SHALL SEE ME AS I REALLY AM AND KNOW THAT YOU BETRAYED THEM.

**WHAT?!!**

NEVER MIND. **MORDONNA** WILL SEE TO IT THAT HER SKURGE DOES NOT SUFFER THE CONSEQUENCES OF HIS ACTIONS.

AN ETERNITY OF PLEASURE HERE IN HEL SHALL BE YOUR REWARD FOR YOUR SERVICES.

I'LL SPLIT YOU WHERE YOU STAND.

NO! I HAVE **NOT** BETRAYED THE ASGARD-IANS!

'TIS NO GOOD, SKURGE. THOR HAS CAUGHT ON NOW! LET ME WHISK MORDONNA AWAY BEFORE HARM COMES TO HER.

**YOU** SHALL BE NEXT.

THOR! YOU MUST BELIEVE ME! I KNEW **NOTHING** OF THIS!

I TRULY THOUGHT I WALKED WITH THE ENCHANTRESS!

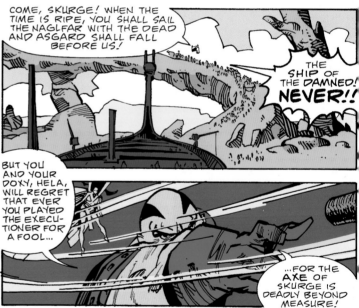

COME, SKURGE! WHEN THE TIME IS RIPE, YOU SHALL SAIL THE NAGLFAR WITH THE DEAD AND ASGARD SHALL FALL BEFORE US!

BUT YOU AND YOUR DOXY, HELA, WILL REGRET THAT EVER YOU PLAYED THE EXECUTIONER FOR A FOOL...

THE SHIP OF THE DAMNED! **NEVER!!**

...FOR THE AXE OF SKURGE IS DEADLY BEYOND MEASURE!

IT CAN CUT THROUGH THE DIMENSIONS THEMSELVES TO RELEASE THE ENERGY THAT BINDS THE NINE WORLDS TOGETHER IN THIS PLACE!!

NOW SHALL CHAOS REIGN IN THIS SPOT AS IT DID IN THE BEGINNING!!!

78

AND FOR A MOMENT, THE BARRIERS BETWEEN THE DIMENSIONS ARE TORN ASUNDER AS THE GREAT AXE CLEAVES THE VERY **FABRIC** OF **INFINITY!**

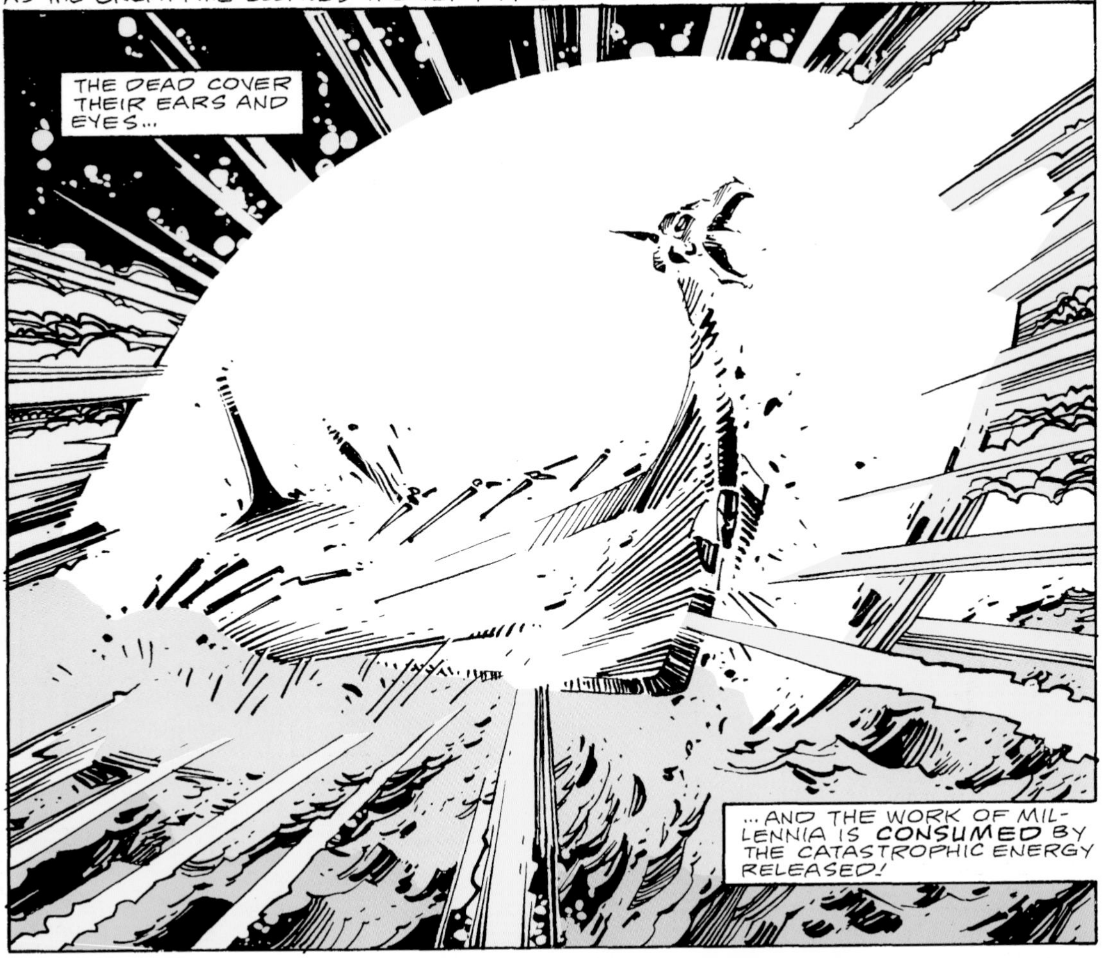
THE DEAD COVER THEIR EARS AND EYES...
...AND THE WORK OF MILLENNIA IS **CONSUMED** BY THE CATASTROPHIC ENERGY RELEASED!

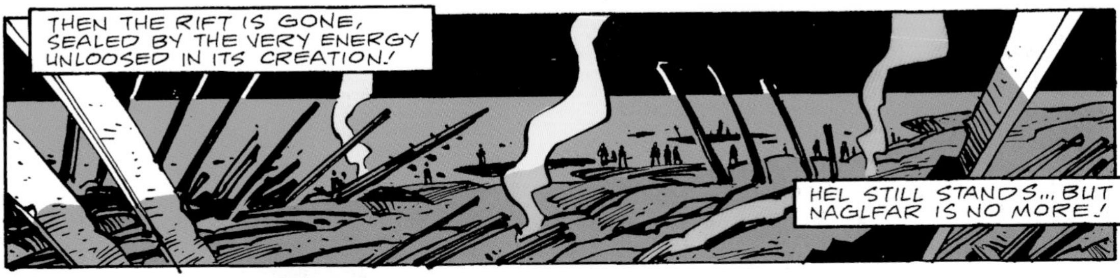
THEN THE RIFT IS GONE, SEALED BY THE VERY ENERGY UNLOOSED IN ITS CREATION!
HEL STILL STANDS... BUT NAGLFAR IS NO MORE!

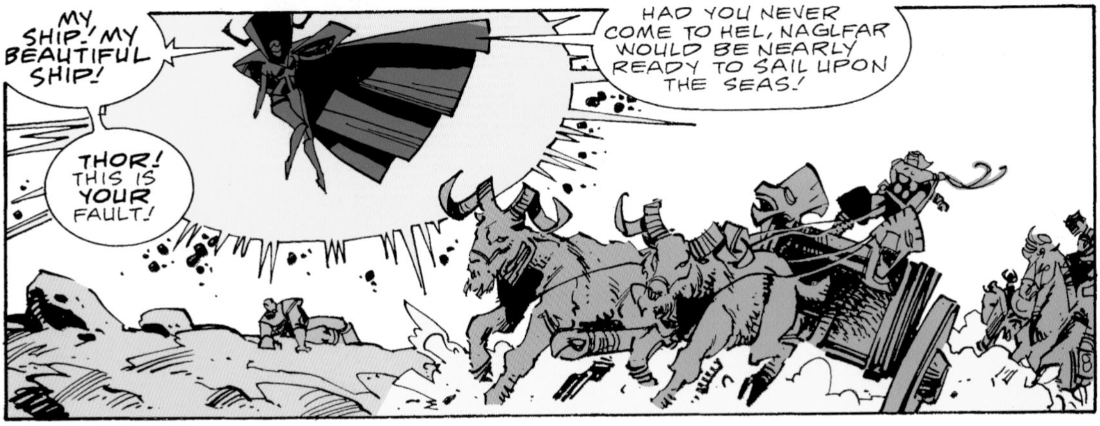
MY SHIP! MY BEAUTIFUL SHIP!
HAD YOU NEVER COME TO HEL, NAGLFAR WOULD BE NEARLY READY TO SAIL UPON THE SEAS!
THOR! THIS IS YOUR FAULT!

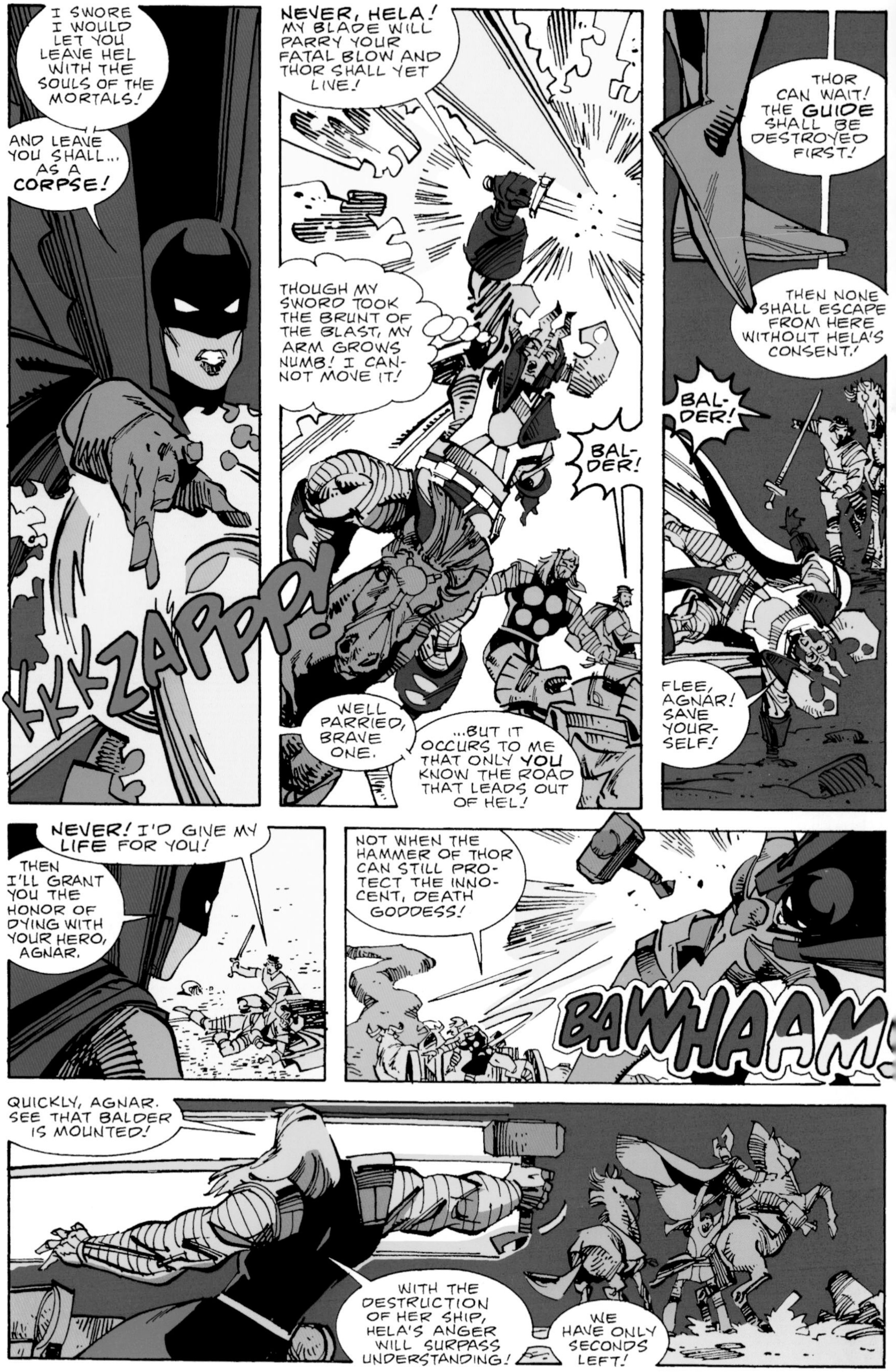

I SWORE I WOULD LET YOU LEAVE HEL WITH THE SOULS OF THE MORTALS!
AND LEAVE YOU SHALL... AS A CORPSE!
KKKZAPPP!
NEVER, HELA! MY BLADE WILL PARRY YOUR FATAL BLOW AND THOR SHALL YET LIVE!
THOUGH MY SWORD TOOK THE BRUNT OF THE BLAST, MY ARM GROWS NUMB! I CAN-NOT MOVE IT!
WELL PARRIED, BRAVE ONE.
...BUT IT OCCURS TO ME THAT ONLY YOU KNOW THE ROAD THAT LEADS OUT OF HEL!
BAL-DER!
THOR CAN WAIT! THE GUIDE SHALL BE DESTROYED FIRST!
THEN NONE SHALL ESCAPE FROM HERE WITHOUT HELA'S CONSENT!
BAL-DER!
FLEE, AGNAR! SAVE YOUR-SELF!
NEVER! I'D GIVE MY LIFE FOR YOU!
THEN I'LL GRANT YOU THE HONOR OF DYING WITH YOUR HERO, AGNAR.
NOT WHEN THE HAMMER OF THOR CAN STILL PRO-TECT THE INNO-CENT, DEATH GODDESS!
BAWHAAM
QUICKLY, AGNAR. SEE THAT BALDER IS MOUNTED!
WITH THE DESTRUCTION OF HER SHIP, HELA'S ANGER WILL SURPASS UNDERSTANDING!
WE HAVE ONLY SECONDS LEFT!

COME, HEROES! TURN YOUR HORSES' HEADS AND FOL-LOW ME!

THE HELWAY LIES BEFORE US AND WE MUST RIDE IT TO FREEDOM...

...THOUGH ALL THE POWERS OF HEL SHOULD SEEK TO BAR OUR WAY!

GET THOSE WAGONS MOV-ING!

AND EVEN AS THE ASGARDIANS DRAW NEAR, THE ROCKS OF HEL BEGIN TO TWIST AND WRITHE LIKE LIVING THINGS...

...AS FROM HER STYGIAN DEPTHS, THE REALM OF DEATH DISGORGES THE **WARRIORS** OF DESPAIR!

HAROKIN, LOOK! THE CREATURES OF HEL ARE RISING!

THEN LET THEM **RISE** INTO THE TEETH OF THE STORM! THE EINHERJAR WERE **BORN** TO FIGHT!

AND I WAS BORN TO LEAD THEM!

THIS IS OUR MOMENT!

THE WEAPONS WE TOOK FROM MIDGARD* SHALL SPEAK TO HELA IN A TONGUE SHE CAN UN-DERSTAND!

CLOSE UP THE RANKS...

AND ON MY SIGNAL...

* THOR 360

**81**

OPEN FIRE!

BUDDA BUDDA BUDDA BUDDA

BLAM! KAPOW! KAPOW

NOW, WARRIORS, SPUR YOUR STEEDS TO THEIR UTMOST!

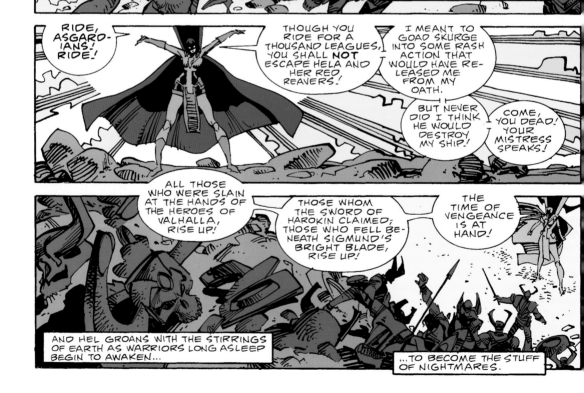

AND THE CREATURES OF HEL ARE THROWN ASIDE BY THE THUNDER-ING HOOVES OF THE EINHERJAR'S HORSES...

...AS THE RIDERS OF ASGARD SLASH THROUGH THE BREACH IN THEIR RANKS!

RIDE, ASGARD-IANS! RIDE!

THOUGH YOU RIDE FOR A THOUSAND LEAGUES, YOU SHALL **NOT** ESCAPE HELA AND HER RED REAVERS!

I MEANT TO GOAD SKURGE INTO SOME RASH ACTION THAT WOULD HAVE RE-LEASED ME FROM MY OATH.

BUT NEVER DID I THINK HE WOULD DESTROY MY SHIP!

COME, YOU DEAD! YOUR MISTRESS SPEAKS!

ALL THOSE WHO WERE SLAIN AT THE HANDS OF THE HEROES OF VALHALLA, RISE UP!

THOSE WHOM THE SWORD OF HAROKIN CLAIMED; THOSE WHO FELL BE-NEATH SIGMUND'S BRIGHT BLADE, RISE UP!

THE TIME OF VENGEANCE IS AT HAND!

AND HEL GROANS WITH THE STIRRINGS OF EARTH AS WARRIORS LONG ASLEEP BEGIN TO AWAKEN...

...TO BECOME THE STUFF OF NIGHTMARES.

AND FAR AHEAD, AS THE ASGARDIANS CONTINUE THEIR CLIMB UP THE HELWAY TOWARD THE SUN...

WHAT IS IT, BALDER? WHY DO YOU PAUSE?

BEFORE US GATHERS A LOWERING CLOUD I HAVE SEEN BEFORE.

LOOK AHEAD, THOR, AND SEE THE FACE OF DEATH.

A SHIELD-WALL, MADE BY THE WARRIORS WE SLEW IN EVERY BATTLE SINCE THE BEGINNING!

THEY STAND AGAINST US IN HATE!

THESE ARE *NOT* THE MEN WE FACED AND FOUGHT, BUT THE SHADOWS OF THOSE MEN IN HELA'S SERVICE NOW!

LOOK TO THY DEFENSES, DENIZENS OF HEL! NEVER AGAIN WILL YOU SEE WARRIORS THE LIKE OF VALHALLA'S FINEST!

EINHERJAR! FOLLOW ME!

WE WILL BREAK THEM HERE OR DIE THE *REAL* DEATH!

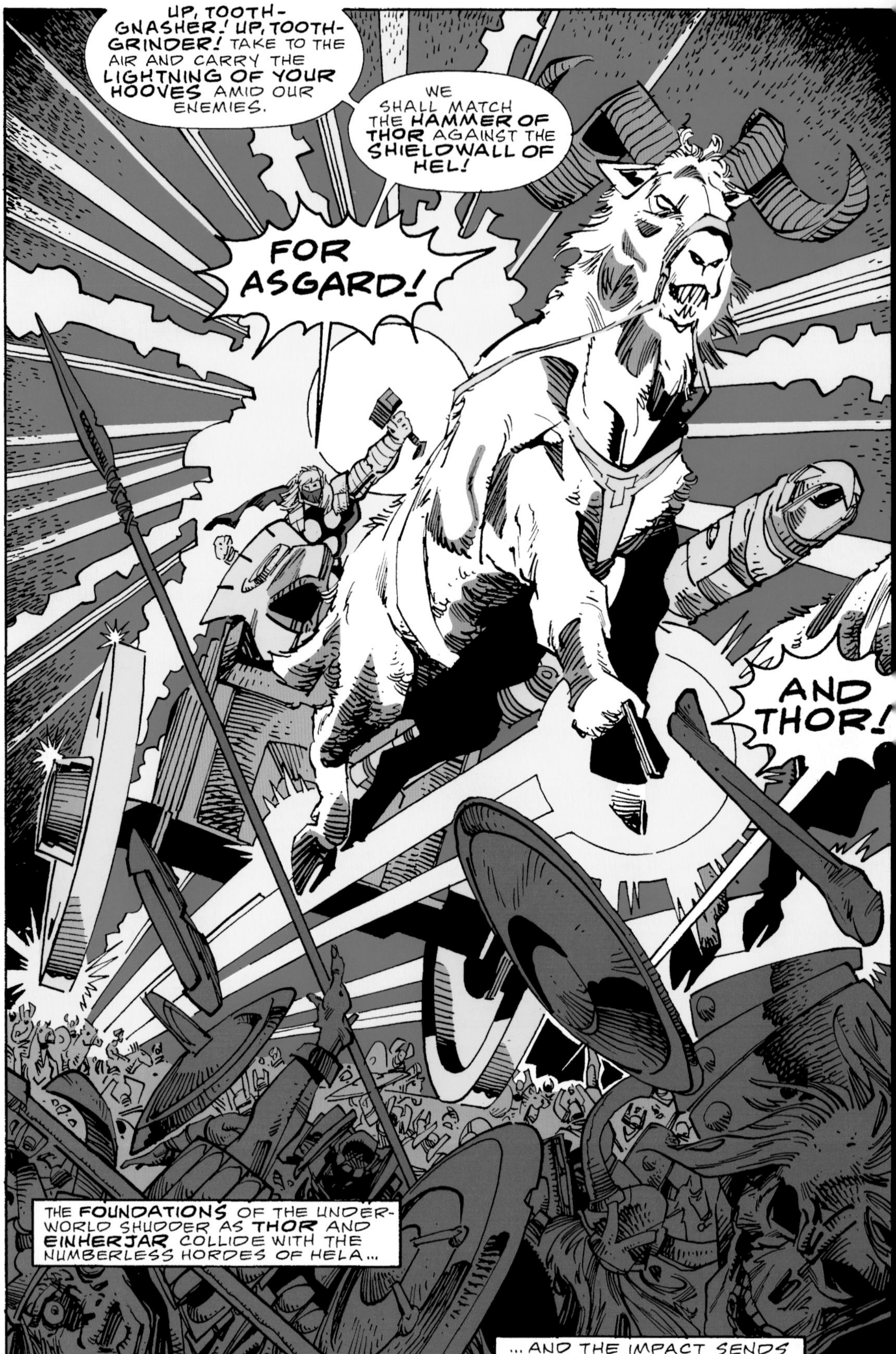
UP, TOOTH-GNASHER! UP, TOOTH-GRINDER! TAKE TO THE AIR AND CARRY THE LIGHTNING OF YOUR HOOVES AMID OUR ENEMIES.
WE SHALL MATCH THE HAMMER OF THOR AGAINST THE SHIELDWALL OF HEL!
FOR ASGARD!
AND THOR!
THE FOUNDATIONS OF THE UNDERWORLD SHUDDER AS THOR AND EINHERJAR COLLIDE WITH THE NUMBERLESS HORDES OF HELA...
...AND THE IMPACT SENDS TREMORS TO THE FURTHEST CORNER OF THE REALM...

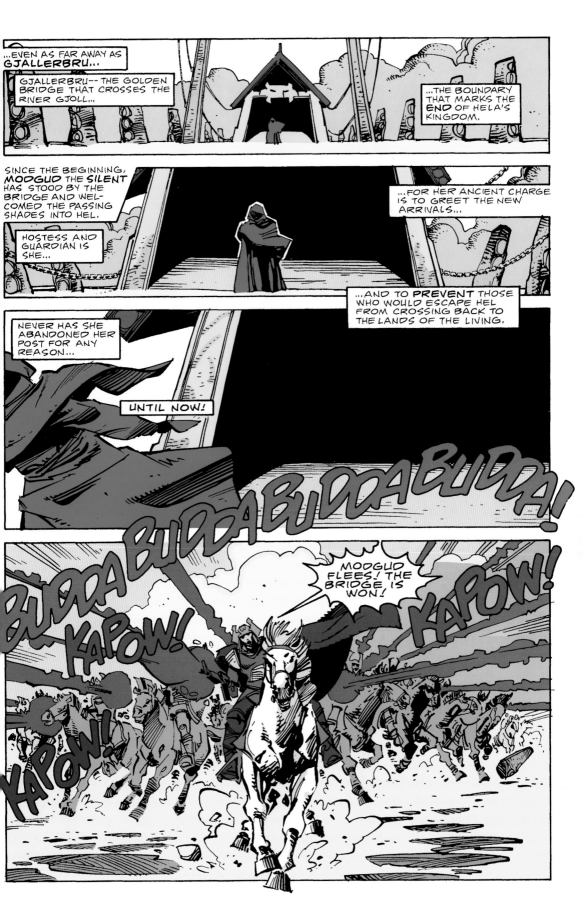

...EVEN AS FAR AWAY AS GJALLERBRU...

GJALLERBRU-- THE GOLDEN BRIDGE THAT CROSSES THE RIVER GJOLL...

...THE BOUNDARY THAT MARKS THE END OF HELA'S KINGDOM.

SINCE THE BEGINNING, MODGUD THE SILENT HAS STOOD BY THE BRIDGE AND WELCOMED THE PASSING SHADES INTO HEL.

...FOR HER ANCIENT CHARGE IS TO GREET THE NEW ARRIVALS...

HOSTESS AND GUARDIAN IS SHE...

...AND TO PREVENT THOSE WHO WOULD ESCAPE HEL FROM CROSSING BACK TO THE LANDS OF THE LIVING.

NEVER HAS SHE ABANDONED HER POST FOR ANY REASON...

UNTIL NOW!

BUDDABUDDABUDDA!

BUDDABUDDA!

KAPOW!

KAPOW!

KAPOW!

MODGUD FLEES! THE BRIDGE IS WON!

BALDER, TO YOU I GIVE THE CHARGE TO SEE THESE MORTAL SOULS SAFELY BACK TO MIDGARD.

WE HAVE ONLY BROKEN THROUGH THE RANKS OF HELA'S WARRIORS.

WE CANNOT TRAVEL QUICKLY THROUGH THE TUNNELS BEYOND THE BRIDGE THAT LEAD TO SAFETY...

...AND SOON ENOUGH ALL OF HEL WILL BE AT OUR HEELS.

WHAT OF YOU?

I WILL STAY **HERE** AND HOLD THEM TILL YOU HAVE HAD TIME TO ESCAPE.

SURELY YOU WILL **PERISH** IN THIS ATTEMPT.

PERHAPS NOT.

MY HAMMER MAY YET WIN ME PASSAGE THROUGH TO THE UPPER WORLDS.

BUT NO ONE ELSE CAN HOLD THE HORDES OF HEL HERE AT THE BRIDGE TILL YOU AND ALL THE OTHERS ARE SAFE.

SUDDENLY FROM OUT OF THE SHADOWS BEHIND THOR...

CRACKK!

NO, THUNDERER!

YOU SHALL **NOT** HOLD THE HORDES OF HEL AT BAY BEFORE THE BRIDGE.

THE EXECU-TIONER!

HE HAS FELLED THOR!

THIS IS SOME TRICK OF THE TRAITOR.

SLAY HIM!

GIVE ME YOUR WEAPON, HAROKIN.

BALDER, HEAR ME OUT.

SPEAK.

THEY MADE A FOOL OF ME, BALDER. THEY LAUGHED AT ME.

EVERYBODY LAUGHS AT SKURGE. HELA, MORDONNA, EVEN THE ENCHANTRESS I LOVE, THEY ALL LAUGH AT ME.

EXCEPT YOU. BALDER IS TOO KIND TO LAUGH AT SKURGE.

BUT WHEN-EVER THEY LAUGH, I HURT INSIDE, MAYBE I DIE A LITTLE.

NOW I THINK I AM DEAD ALREADY.

AND MY AXE WAS DESTROYED WITH NAGLFAR.

SO I WILL STAY BEHIND AND THE LAST LAUGH WILL BE MINE.

YOU AND THOR HAVE A DRINK WHEN YOU ARE NEXT IN ASGARD AND LAUGH SKURGE'S LAST LAUGH TO-GETHER.

I WILL HOLD THE BRIDGE.

87

IN THE DISTANCE, THERE IS THUNDER IN THE AIR.

LEAVE ME AS MUCH AMMUNITION AS YOU CAN SPARE AND AN EXTRA WEAPON OR TWO.

AND BID THOR FAREWELL FOR ME.

TELL HIM I AM SORRY I STRUCK HIM UNFAIRLY.

WE SHALL HAVE THAT DRINK, HE AND I.

MOUNT UP, YOU WARRIORS, AND RIDE!

GOODBYE, BALDER.

THE THUNDER IS LOUDER NOW.

... AND SKURGE IS WAITING.

PERHAPS HE HAS WAITED ALL HIS LIFE FOR THIS ONE MOMENT.

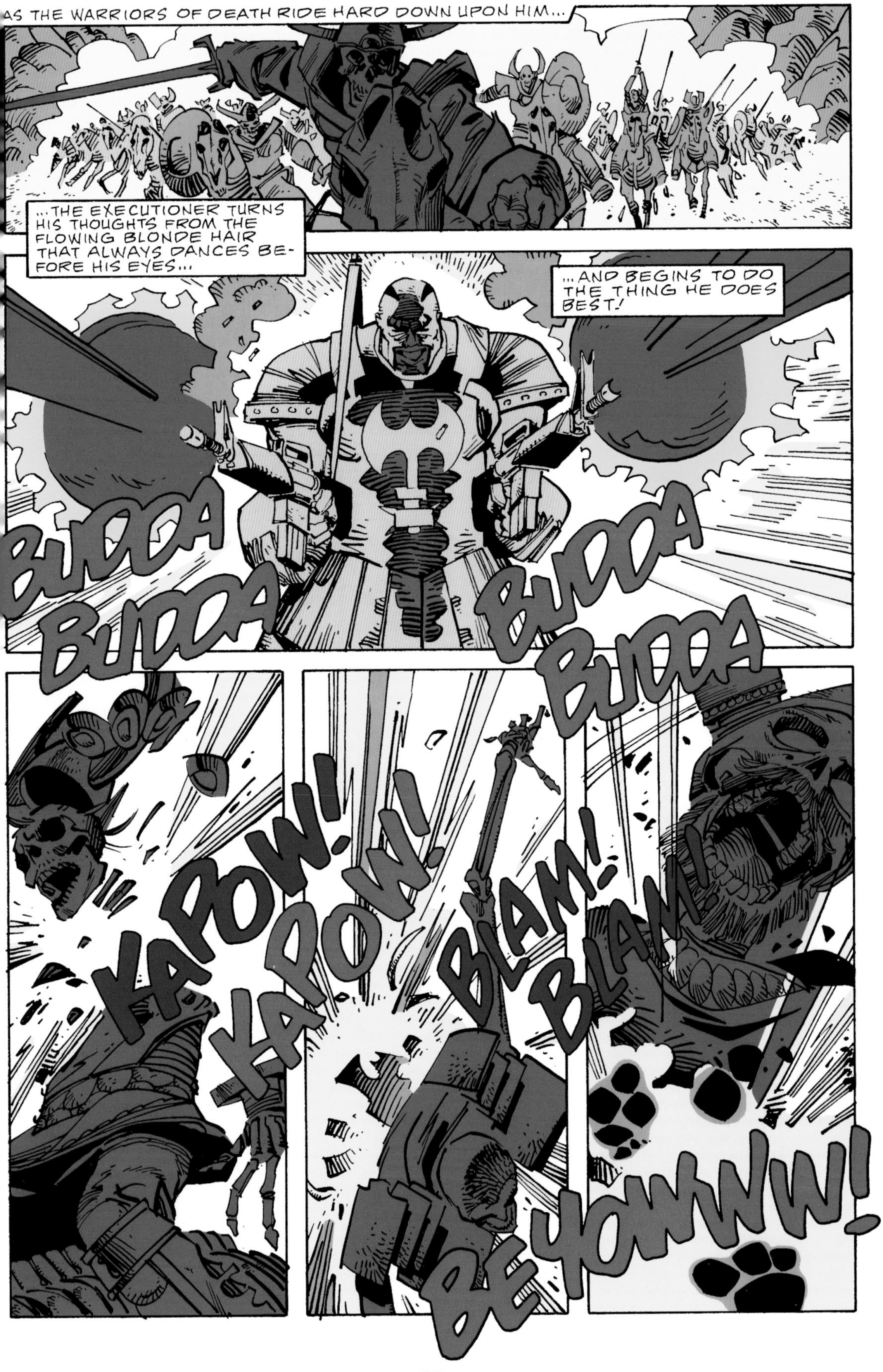
AS THE WARRIORS OF DEATH RIDE HARD DOWN UPON HIM...
...THE EXECUTIONER TURNS HIS THOUGHTS FROM THE FLOWING BLONDE HAIR THAT ALWAYS DANCES BEFORE HIS EYES...
...AND BEGINS TO DO THE THING HE DOES BEST!
BUDDA BUDDA
BUDDA BUDDA
KAPOW! KAPOW!
BLAM! BLAM!
BEYOWWW!

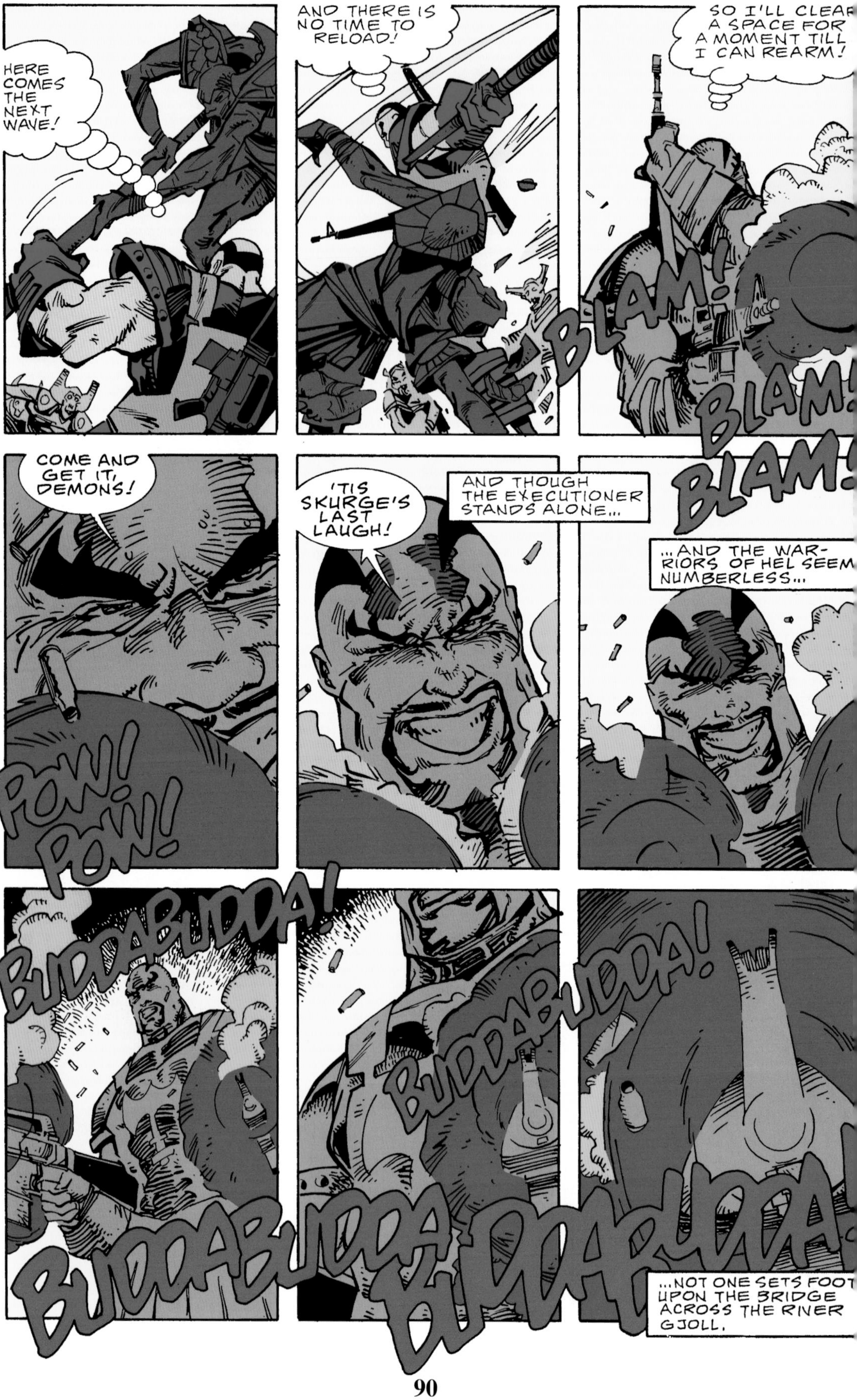
HERE COMES THE NEXT WAVE!
AND THERE IS NO TIME TO RELOAD!
SO I'LL CLEAR A SPACE FOR A MOMENT TILL I CAN REARM!
BLAM!
BLAM!
BLAM!
COME AND GET IT, DEMONS!
POW! POW!
'TIS SKURGE'S LAST LAUGH!
AND THOUGH THE EXECUTIONER STANDS ALONE...
...AND THE WARRIORS OF HEL SEEM NUMBERLESS...
BUDDABUDDA!
BUDDABUDDA!
BUDDABUDDA
BUDDABUDDA
...NOT ONE SETS FOOT UPON THE BRIDGE ACROSS THE RIVER GJOLL.

THEY SING NO SONGS IN HEL, NOR DO THEY CELEBRATE HEROES...

HE STOOD ALONE AT GJALLERBRU...

...FOR SILENT IS THAT DISMAL REALM AND CHEERLESS...

...BUT THE STORY OF THE GJALLERBRU AND THE GOD WHO DEFENDED IT IS WHISPERED ACROSS THE NINE WORLDS...

...AND WHEN A NEW ARRIVAL ASKS ABOUT THE ONE TO WHOM EVEN HELA BOWS HER HEAD...

...THE ANSWER IS ALWAYS THE SAME...

...AND THAT ANSWER IS ENOUGH.

91

BALDER, WHAT HAPPENED?

SKURGE! HE TOOK YOUR PLACE, THOR. HE HAS GIVEN UP HIS LIFE THAT WE MAY WIN FREE.

BUT HE HELD THE BRIDGE; THERE IS NO LONGER ANY PURSUIT.

THEN HE HAS DONE WHAT I WOULD HAVE DONE!

I THOUGHT IN BATTLE I MIGHT EASE THE TORMENT OF MY WOUNDS!

BUT I SEE THAT SKURGE'S NEED WAS GREATER!

I AM NOT FATED TO FIND RESPITE SO EASILY, SO BE IT.

WHERE ARE WE?

SOMEHOW, THE WAY OUT IS NOT SO LONG AND DARK AS IT WAS ON OUR JOURNEY DOWN.

BEFORE US LIES THE CAVE EXIT.

PERHAPS HELA HAS SPED US ON OUR WAY TO MEET THE HEL HOUND, GARM, WHO STANDS IN THE VALLEY BEYOND...

...HOPING HE WILL DO WHAT HER WARRIORS COULD NOT!

LEAP YOU TO THE SADDLE AGAIN, BALDER!

THE EXECUTIONER HAS FOUGHT ONE FIGHT FOR ME ALREADY!

THIS BATTLE IS MINE!

THOR IS CRACKLING WITH ENERGY!

I THINK PERHAPS THAT GARM HAD BEST BEWARE!

SO ODINSON! YOU HAVE GOTTEN THIS FAR AND NOT UNSCATHED I SEE.

BUT I WILL FEAST UPON YOUR BONES! THEN TRULY SHALL I BE KNOWN AS THE DOOM OF THOR!

CRATHAAHMM!!

FOOL-ISH HOUND!

SKURGE IS DEAD! I AM WOUNDED! AND MANY OF THE EINHERJAR WHO RODE WITH US TO HEL WILL NOT RIDE OUT AGAIN!

BUT HELD BY YOUR CHAIN, YOU ARE A STATIONARY TARGET!

AND TODAY, YOU ARE NO MATCH FOR THOR!

GNASSHH!

TURN, GARM, AND FACE THE UNLEASHED FURY OF THE GOD OF THUNDER!

KARAKATHOOOM!

93

AS EVER, MJOL-NIR RETURNS TO MY HAND AFTER THE BLOW IS STRUCK!

BUT THERE IS NO NEED TO STRIKE AGAIN. GORM LIES STUNNED.

...FOR IN THE SPINNING OF THE WORLD'S TALE, HE HAS SOME PART YET TO PLAY.

'TIS FORTUNATE THAT IN MY WRATH I DID NOT SLAY THE HEL HOUND...

COME, BALDER. COME, HAROKIN. COME, ALL YE WHO WOULD VENTURE FORTH FROM HEL.

THE WAY IS OPEN.

AND INTO THE BRILLIANT SUNLIGHT BURST THE RIDERS OF ASGARD...

...FILLING THEIR LUNGS WITH THE FRESH CLEAN AIR...

...AND SAVORING THE TASTE OF FREEDOM ONCE AGAIN.

94

THE WAGONS ARE HITCHED BEHIND YOUR CHARIOT, MY LORD THOR.

ARE YOU **SURE** YOU DO NOT WISH US TO RIDE WITH YOU TO MIDGARD?

THERE IS NO NEED, HAROKIN,

AND BESIDES, NOW THAT THE RAINBOW BRIDGE IS GONE, YOU WOULD NOT FIND THE ROAD TO EARTH SO EASY AS IT WAS.

BUT MY HAMMER AND MY CHARIOT WILL SEE THE WAGONS THROUGH.

THEN THE EINHERJAR AND I WILL RETURN TO ASGARD TO AWAIT YOU.

DO NOT BE LONG.

FOR SURELY LOKI IS ALREADY PREPARING TO FILL YOUR FATHER'S THRONE AND BECOME ASGARD'S NEW LORD.

I WOULD HATE TO HAVE ESCAPED HEL IN ORDER TO BOW TO LOKI'S SUZERAINTY.

I'LL BE HOME DIRECTLY.

FARE YOU WELL. AND THANKS.

AND YOU, OLD FRIEND. I SEE YOU DO NOT DEPART WITH THE EINHERJAR ON THE ROAD TO ASGARD.

NORN-REALM IS MY DESTINATION, THOR.

I SAID I WOULD RETURN TO KARNILLA IF I SURVIVED.

BUT I AM SORRY TO HAVE COME ON THIS JOURNEY.

I LOVE ALL THAT LIVE, THOR...

...YET IN HELA'S HALLS, THERE ARE WARRIORS WHO ONCE BREATHED THE AIR AS I DO NOW.

I HAVE SEEN NANNA WHOM I ONCE DID LOVE CORRUPTED BY THE KISS OF DEATH*...

...AND I BEGIN TO WONDER IF MY TOUCH IS DOOMED TO BLIGHT THE LIVES OF ALL I CARE FOR.

THE SWORD IS AN EVIL GIFT TO THE LIVING.

*LAST ISSUE.

95

STAY WITH HIM, AGNAR. I FEAR IN HIS PRESENT MOOD, HE NEEDS LOOKING AFTER.

I WILL. A SAFE JOURNEY TO MIDGARD, MY LORD.

AND FEAR NOT. KARNILLA WILL REMEDY HIS BLACKNESS.

IN TRUTH, I HOPE SO.

IT SEEMS WE HAVE **ALL** RETURNED FROM HEL BEARING SCARS.

BEFORE WE LEFT ASGARD, SKURGE SAID TO ME, "YOU WILL NOT REGRET IT" WHEN HE ASKED TO COME ALONG.

HE WAS WRONG.

AND YET WE OWE HIM OUR LIVES, PERHAPS OUR VERY SOULS.

YOUR SACRIFICE WILL NOT BE FORGOTTEN IN ASGARD, WARRIOR,

AND BALDER AND I WILL DRINK YOUR TOAST.

BUT THESE MORTALS WILL NOT REMEMBER YOU.

SHORN OF WILL AND THOUGHT AS THEY ARE NOW...

...ALL THIS SHALL SEEM MERELY A DREAM WHEN THEY HAVE BEEN RETURNED TO THEIR PROPER BODIES.

AND THE SACRIFICES OF THOSE WHO MADE IT POSSIBLE WILL BE FOREVER UNKNOWN TO THEM,

FOR SUCH IS THE WAY OF THE GODS.

AND NOW, MJOLNIR, SPIN A DIMENSION SPANNING VORTEX TO MIDGARD!

...AND LET US TAKE THESE WANDERING SOULS HOME!

AND IF IN THE FORESTS ON THE EDGE OF HEL, THE BIRDS STILL SING...

...THERE IS NO ONE LEFT TO HEAR THEIR SONG.

NEXT: **THIS KURSÉD EARTH...!**
IN WHICH **SECRET WARS II** CONTINUES AND **THOR** CLASHES WITH AN UNBEATABLE FOE (AND GETS TO MEET **POWER PACK**, TOO!).
(IF WE HAD ANY MORE STUFF GOING ON, WE'D HAVE TO START A WHOLE NEW LINE OF COMICS!)

**A**ND FOLLOW THE ADVENTURES OF BALDER UPON HIS RETURN TO NORNREALM IN **BALDER THE BRAVE No. 2** WHERE THINGS ARE NOT WHAT THEY USED TO BE! **BALDER THE BETRAYED!!**

#2 IN A FOUR-ISSUE LIMITED SERIES

# BALDER™
## THE ~~BRAVE~~
### *BETRAYED!*

THE
GOOD
DIE
YOUNG!

7-15-85

N**ORNKEEP**, THE ANCIENT FASTNESS OF THE **QUEEN OF THE NORN REALM**...WELL BEYOND THE BORDERS OF ETERNAL ASGARD.

AND ON THE BALCONY WHERE SHE SPOKE HER ANGRY FAREWELLS TO **BALDER THE BRAVE** LIES **KARNILLA**, BROODING OVER BALDER'S DEPARTURE...

...AND PRAYING FOR HIS **SAFE** RETURN.

THE DAYS HAVE TURNED INTO **WEEKS** AND STILL NO WORD.

IS IT **POSSIBLE** THAT BALDER HAS BEEN **SLAIN** IN HIS FOOLHARDY DESCENT INTO HEL WITH THOR *...

...OR COULD IT BE THAT HE HAS DECIDED **NEVER** TO RETURN TO THE WOMAN WHO CLAIMS TO **LOVE** HIM SO PASSIONATELY...

...BUT COULD NOT EVEN BRING HERSELF TO BID HIM FAREWELL AS HE RODE OFF INTO THE LAND OF DEATH...

...NOR AID HIM IN HIS HOUR OF NEED!

**STan Lee** PRESENTS:

# BALDER THE BETRAYED!

*DETAILS OF THAT ADVENTURE ARE BEING CHRONICLED IN THOR#360-362, OH BEST BELOVED!--RALPH-ETH.

WRITTEN BY **WALTER SIMONSON**   ILLUSTRATED BY **SAL BUSCEMA**   LETTERED BY **JOHN WORKMAN JR.**
COLORED BY **PAUL BECTON**   EDITED BY **RALPH MACCHIO**   EDITOR-IN-CHIEF: **JIM SHOOTER**

WITHIN MY ARMORY IS A **WEAPON** WITH WHICH HE COULD HAVE WON THROUGH ANY DANGER...

...AND I IN MY PRIDE GAVE HIM NOTHING BUT **SCORN** AS HE DEPARTED...

OH, KARNILLA, FOOLISH QUEEN, WHAT BOOTS PRIDE WHEN THE ONE THING YOU LOVE IN ALL THE NINE WORLDS HAS GONE INTO A PLACE SO EVIL...

...WITHOUT EVEN A TOUCH FROM YOU TO SAY "COME BACK TO ME!"

SURELY THERE IS NO GREATER FOOL THAN A FOOL IN LOVE.

GNNGHHNG!!

LEAVE THEM **BE!**

THE BIRDS SING HERE NOW ONLY BECAUSE THIS PLACE WAS ONCE GRACED BY BALDER'S BEAUTY.

NOW THAT HE IS GONE, THEY ARE ALL I HAVE LEFT OF HIM.

TOUCH THEM ON YOUR PERIL!

IF YOU HAD SUNG SO SWEETLY, PERHAPS YOUR TONGUE WOULD STILL WAG WITHIN YOUR HEAD!

GUGG-GGNB!

WHAT IS IT, VARTHOG?

GAGG-GGNG!

BUT IT IS! **BALDER** HAS **RETURNED** FROM HEL **ALIVE!!**

A LONE HORSEMAN! SURELY IT CANNOT BE!

99

GUARDS! OPEN WIDE THE PORTALS! BALDER THE BRAVE HAS RETURNED TO NORNKEEP!

BALDER! MY DEAREST!

AND THE THUNDERING HOOFS STRIKE SPARKS UPON THE STONE FLAGGING AS THE GRACEFUL FIGURE ALIGHTS...

...AND KARNILLA FINDS HERSELF SWEPT UP IN THE ARMS OF HER ONE TRUE LOVE.

HOLD ME TIGHTLY, BALDER!

I WANT TO FEEL AS THOUGH I SHALL NEVER LOSE YOU AGAIN!

REST ASSURED, MY DARLING, I SHALL NEVER LET YOU GO!!

MY LOVE! FORBEAR A LITTLE, YOUR EMBRACE FAIRLY CRUSHES ME TO YOUR BREAST!

BALDER?!

MMM-MPH!

WHAT'S HAPPEN-ING?

HIS ARMS!!

I CAN-NOT BREATHE!

...

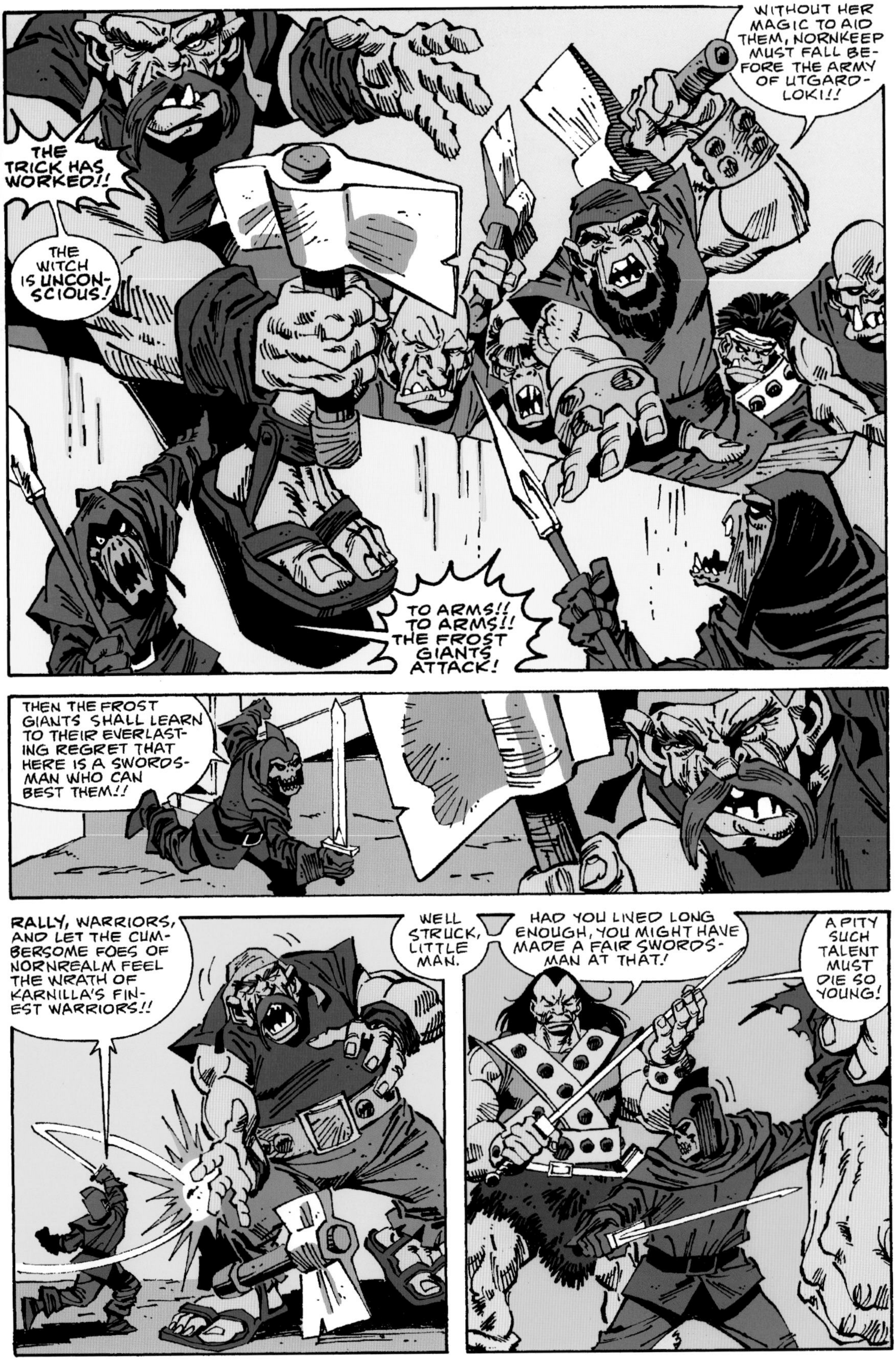
THE TRICK HAS WORKED!!
THE WITCH IS UNCONSCIOUS!
WITHOUT HER MAGIC TO AID THEM, NORNKEEP MUST FALL BEFORE THE ARMY OF UTGARD-LOKI!!
TO ARMS!! TO ARMS!! THE FROST GIANTS ATTACK!
THEN THE FROST GIANTS SHALL LEARN TO THEIR EVERLASTING REGRET THAT HERE IS A SWORDSMAN WHO CAN BEST THEM!!
RALLY, WARRIORS, AND LET THE CUMBERSOME FOES OF NORNREALM FEEL THE WRATH OF KARNILLA'S FINEST WARRIORS!!
WELL STRUCK, LITTLE MAN.
HAD YOU LIVED LONG ENOUGH, YOU MIGHT HAVE MADE A FAIR SWORDSMAN AT THAT!
A PITY SUCH TALENT MUST DIE SO YOUNG!

HOW DID YOU COME TO BE CALLED THE **FROST GIANTS** AND NOT THE **WIND GIANTS,** BRAGGART!!

TO ME, KINSMEN!

NOT ALL THY CLAN CAN SAVE YOU FROM THE SWIFT SWORD OF HAGEN!

GAGG-GGKK!

Swicckkkkk!

I HAVE NO EQUAL WITH A BLADE IN THE NINE WORLDS...

...AND THESE FEW DEMONS SHALL BE DISPATCHED BEFORE I NEED TO DRAW A BREATH!

BE GRATEFUL FOR YOUR FATE, WARRIORS OF KARNILLA, AS YOU TREAD THE DUSTY ROAD TO HEL!

FOR YOUR TIME IN THIS WORLD IS FINISHED!

BUT YOUR MISTRESS SHALL WISH SHE HAD DIED WITH YOU 'ERE WE ARE FINISHED WITH HER!

HE HAS FELLED OUR FINEST FIGHT-ERS SINGLE-HANDED!

LET US FLEE!!

WAIT! WHAT SHADOW FALLS ACROSS THE COURT-YARD?

'TIS THE SHADOW, LITTLE ONES, OF **UTGARD-LOKI,** RULER OF THE FROST GIANTS!!

THEY SAY THE SANDMAN'S MAGIC SAND BRINGS SLEEP!

BUT THE DUST OF UTGARD-LOKI BRINGS SOMETHING BETTER!

NO LONGER ARE YOU THE GUARDIANS OF THE NORN-REALM!

NOW YOU MIGHT BETTER BE CALLED ITS "BEDROCK"!!!

HAHAHA HAHAHAHA HAHA!!

AND AS THE SOUND OF UTGARD-LOKI'S BALEFUL LAUGHTER SPREADS ACROSS THE LAND...

...SO, TOO, DOES THE MAGIC DUST UNTIL AT LAST, IN A KINGDOM FILLED WITH MONU-MENTS OF STONE...

...EVERY SOUND OF LIFE IS STILLED!

IT IS THE STILLNESS OF THE GRAVE.

NOW, YOU BLACKGUARDS! MOVE!

I SENSE SOME **OBJECT** OF **POWER** HIDDEN WITH-IN THIS CASTLE!

AND WHATEVER KARNILLA HAS HID-DEN AWAY FROM PRYING EYES MUST BE VALUABLE INDEED!

SEARCH THE CASTLE!

AND SEARCH IT THEY DO...

...FROM TOPMOST GARRET, TO DARKEST DUNGEON AS THE HOURS WEAR AWAY...

...TILL FROM DEEP WITHIN THE VERY BOWELS OF THE FORTRESS...

THE TREASURE IS OURS!!

**103**

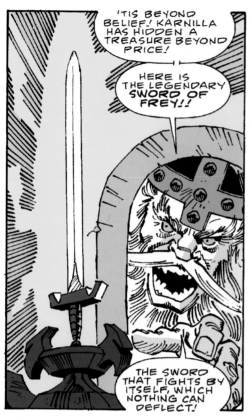

'TIS BEYOND BELIEF! KARNILLA HAS HIDDEN A TREASURE BEYOND PRICE!

HERE IS THE LEGENDARY SWORD OF FREY!!

THE SWORD THAT FIGHTS BY ITSELF, WHICH NOTHING CAN DEFLECT!

HAGEN, STEP FORTH! THIS PRIZE WE SHALL BESTOW ON YOU.

WITH THIS WEAPON, EVEN THE GODS WILL FEAR YOU...

...AND THE GIANTS SHALL BE UNVANQUISHABLE!

NOW WHAT OF KARNILLA?

"GRUNGNIR, THE SHAPE-CHANGER, IS BINDING HER WITH THE MAGIC SHACKLES, LORD.

"NO LONGER WILL SHE BE ABLE TO WORK HER SPELLS.

"INSTEAD, OUR EVERY WHIM WILL BE HER LAW!"

MMMMPH!

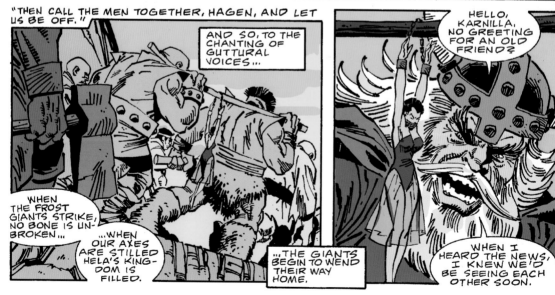

"THEN CALL THE MEN TOGETHER, HAGEN, AND LET US BE OFF."

AND SO, TO THE CHANTING OF GUTTURAL VOICES...

WHEN THE FROST GIANTS STRIKE, NO BONE IS UNBROKEN...

...WHEN OUR AXES ARE STILLED HELA'S KINGDOM IS FILLED.

...THE GIANTS BEGIN TO WEND THEIR WAY HOME,

HELLO, KARNILLA, NO GREETING FOR AN OLD FRIEND?

WHEN I HEARD THE NEWS, I KNEW WE'D BE SEEING EACH OTHER SOON.

104

"BUT I AM GETTING AHEAD OF MY STORY."

UTGARD-LOKI!! OLD ONE-EYE IS GONE FOREVER!

"'TWAS NOT LONG AGO THAT TWO OF MY SUBJECTS RETURNED FROM WANDERING ABOUT IN THE WIDE WORLD."

SPEAK PLAINLY, YURTHAGG!! WHAT DO YOU MEAN?

ODIN BROADHAT IS GONE! ASGARD IS WITHOUT A RULER NOW.

IF THIS IS TRUE, THEN THE TIME TO DESTROY THE GOLDEN REALM IS AT HAND!

BUT WE MUST BE CAREFUL. WE SHALL STRIKE SECRETLY AT HER ALLIES FIRST!

NO WORD OF WHAT WE DO MUST BE CARRIED TO ASGARD UNTIL IT IS TOO LATE FOR HER TO SAVE HERSELF!

AND NOW, MY DEAR, WE HAVE ACCOMPLISHED THE FIRST STEP IN THE CONQUEST OF ASGARD.

ONE BY ONE HER ALLIES WILL BE ELIMINATED...

...UNTIL, AT LAST, THE GOLDEN REALM SHALL FACE THE FULL MIGHT OF JOTUNHEIM ALONE...

...AND FALL.

WELCOME TO YOUR NEW HOME, KARNILLA.

SOME TIME LATER, ON THE OUTSKIRTS OF THE NORN REALM, A PAIR OF TRAVELERS RIDE IN SILENCE ACROSS THE DESOLATE COUNTRYSIDE...

SINCE OUR DEPARTURE FROM HEL, BALDER HAS SPOKEN NO MORE THAN THREE WORDS.

OUR FINAL STRUGGLE TO ESCAPE THE GRIP OF HELA ONLY SERVED TO REMIND BALDER HOW TERRIBLE IS THE FATE OF THOSE HE HAS SLAIN IN THE PAST.

A WARRIOR DIES ONLY **ONCE** IN BATTLE...HE DIES A **THOUSAND** TIMES IN HEL.

AND THOUGH BALDER BEARS HIS OWN WOUNDS WITH FORTITUDE...

...THE HURTS OF THE MIND MAY BE BEYOND EVEN KARNILLA'S HEALING TOUCH.

I PRAY IT IS NOT SO.

AT LAST, BRAVE BALDER, WE HAVE REACHED THE BOUNDARIES OF THE NORN REALM.

HERE YOU WILL CERTAINLY FIND THE PEACE AND SANCTUARY YOU--!

BALDER! THE **CROPS!** THE SUN HAS SCORCHED THEM IN THE FIELDS!

AND WHO WOULD PLANT A STONE STATUE AS A SCARECROW?

LOOK AGAIN, AGNAR.

THESE ARE **NOT** STONE STATUES...

...BUT THE VERY **INHABITANTS** OF THE REALM.

LET US MAKE ALL HASTE FOR NORN-KEEP.

SOME-THING IS SORELY AMISS IN THE KING-DOM!

106

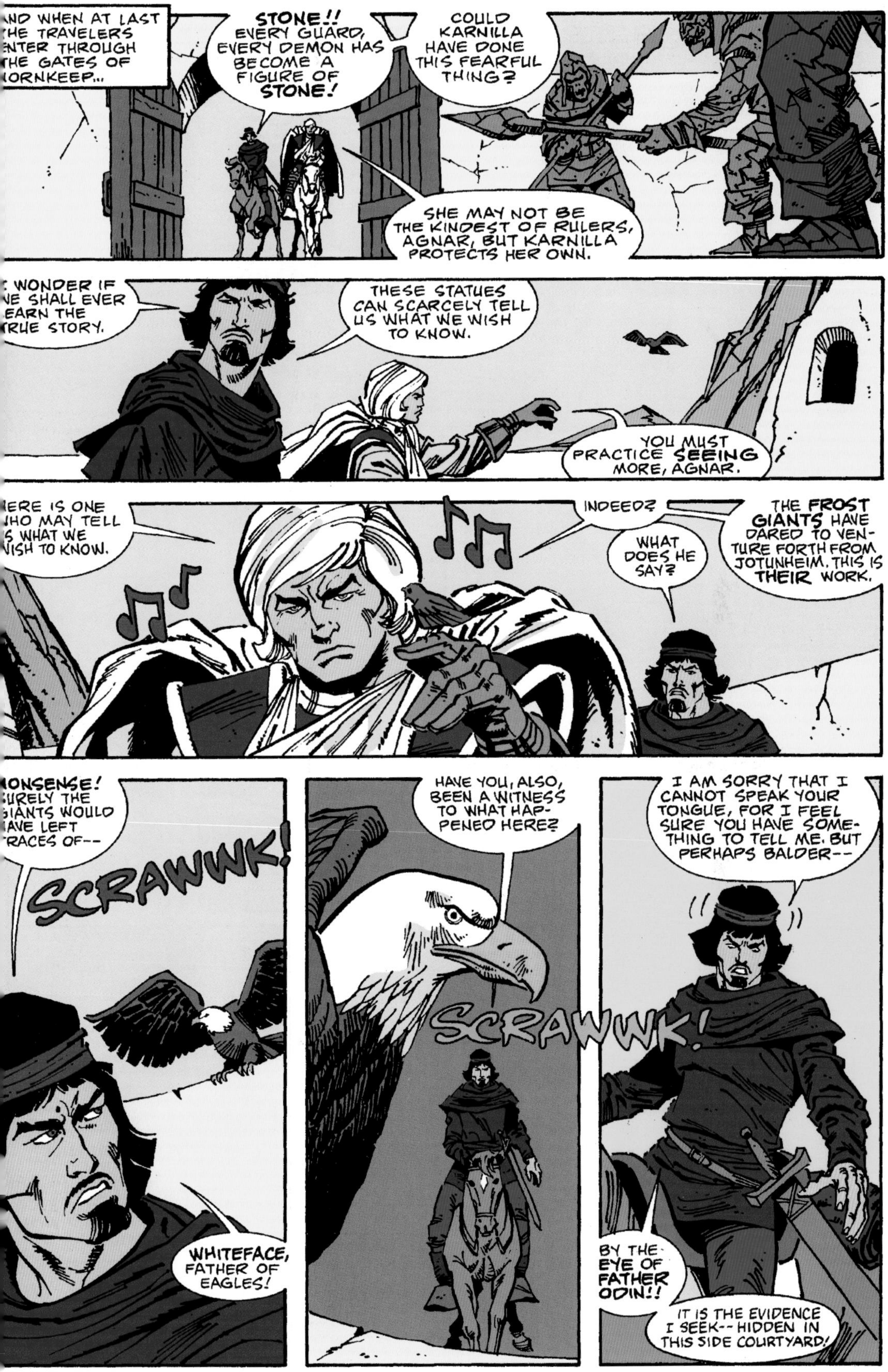

AND WHEN AT LAST THE TRAVELERS ENTER THROUGH THE GATES OF NORNKEEP...
STONE!! EVERY GUARD, EVERY DEMON HAS BECOME A FIGURE OF STONE!
COULD KARNILLA HAVE DONE THIS FEARFUL THING?
SHE MAY NOT BE THE KINDEST OF RULERS, AGNAR, BUT KARNILLA PROTECTS HER OWN.
I WONDER IF WE SHALL EVER LEARN THE TRUE STORY.
THESE STATUES CAN SCARCELY TELL US WHAT WE WISH TO KNOW.
YOU MUST PRACTICE SEEING MORE, AGNAR.
HERE IS ONE WHO MAY TELL US WHAT WE WISH TO KNOW.
INDEED?
WHAT DOES HE SAY?
THE FROST GIANTS HAVE DARED TO VENTURE FORTH FROM JOTUNHEIM. THIS IS THEIR WORK.
NONSENSE! SURELY THE GIANTS WOULD HAVE LEFT TRACES OF--
SCRAWWK!
WHITEFACE, FATHER OF EAGLES!
HAVE YOU, ALSO, BEEN A WITNESS TO WHAT HAPPENED HERE?
SCRAWWK!
I AM SORRY THAT I CANNOT SPEAK YOUR TONGUE, FOR I FEEL SURE YOU HAVE SOMETHING TO TELL ME. BUT PERHAPS BALDER--
BY THE EYE OF FATHER ODIN!!
IT IS THE EVIDENCE I SEEK--HIDDEN IN THIS SIDE COURTYARD!

**BALDER! LOOK! THE LITTLE BIRD WAS RIGHT!**

I MAY NEED TO PRACTICE SEEING BUT **THIS** IS BIG ENOUGH THAT EVEN I CAN SEE IT.

WITH ONLY A LITTLE HELP FROM WHITE-FACE.

BUT HERE IS SOMETHING THAT I HAVE FOUND WITHOUT HIS AID.

WHAT IS IT?

KARNILLA'S HAIR... SHE HAS BEEN SHORN BY HER CAPTORS... THEY HAVE TAKEN HER AS **SLAVE.**

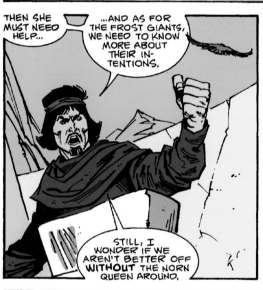

THEN SHE MUST NEED HELP...

...AND AS FOR THE FROST GIANTS, WE NEED TO KNOW MORE ABOUT THEIR INTENTIONS.

STILL, I WONDER IF WE AREN'T **BETTER** OFF **WITHOUT** THE NORN QUEEN AROUND.

THOUGH YOU MAY NOT APPROVE OF HER, KARNILLA CAME TO ASGARD'S AID AGAINST THE FORCES OF SURTUR...✳

✳THOR 352--R.M.

...AND WOULD NO REFUSE SUCCOR TO ANY ONE IN NEED.

YOUR **FIRST** IMPULSE WAS THE TRUE ONE, AGNAR.

AND SHORTLY, WHEN THE TWO WARRIORS HAVE REPROVISIONED THEMSELVES FROM THE KEEP...

NOW LET THE GIANTS OF JOTUNHEIM BEWARE.

THEY WILL LEARN THAT NEITHER ASGAR NOR HER ALLIES MAY BE ATTACKED WITH IMPUNITY!

BALDER!

WHITEFACE! HOW IS IT WITH YOU, FRIEND?

SCRAWWK! AWWWK!

SEE HOW HE WHEELS TO THE **EAST** TOWARD JOTUNHEIM.

HE WOULD GUIDE US TO THE ENEMY.

IT HARDLY SEEMS NECESSARY THAT WE SHALL NEED SUCH SHARP EYES TO FOLLOW THE TRACES OF GIANTS.

THEY WILL HAVE LEFT THEIR MARK ALL ALONG THEIR ROAD.

PERHAPS, AGNAR, BUT REMEMBER HOW **YOUR** EYES NEEDED HELP IN NORNKEEP.

AND IN THEIR OWN KINGDOM, THE GIANTS' POWER WILL BE STRONG.

WHITEFACE WISHES TO BE OUR GUIDE AND I WOULD NOT SAY HIM NAY...

..EVEN IF I COULD SEE EVERY FOOTPRINT AND BROKEN TREE FROM HERE TO JOTUNHEIM.

BUT COME. TIME IS PRECIOUS AND WITH EVERY PASSING MOMENT, WE COULD BE ONE STEP CLOSER TO KARNILLA AND HER ABDUCTORS.

AND INTO THE EAST, THE RIDERS DIMINISH UNTIL AT LAST...

...EVEN THE DUST OF THEIR PASSING HAS BEEN BLOWN AWAY BY THE WIND, LEAVING NOT A TRACE BEHIND.

MEANWHILE, IN THE ICY WASTES OF JOTUNHEIM, IN THE FORTRESS OF UT-GARD-LOKI...

KEEP WORKING, SLAVE! THERE ARE THREE HUNDRED **MORE** ROOMS TO BE DONE!

THE MIGHTY NORN QUEEN SHALL LIVE OUT HER DAYS AS A SIMPLE DRUDGE...

HAR! HAR!

...FIT ONLY TO SCOUR STONES AND WIPE OUR FEET!

SO DO THE GIANTS SERVE THEIR ENEMIES.

LAUGH NOW, YOU CLODS OF LITTLE IMAGINATION!

SOME DAY, KARNILLA WILL BE FREE OF THESE SHACKLES AND WHEN THAT DAY COMES...

...HER HEART SHALL BE AS HARD AS THESE STONES!

NOW WHAT, BALDER? THE WAY ENDS HERE AGAINST BOTTOMLESS CLIFFS.

THE **EASY** ROAD ENDS HERE, AGNAR. THE WAY GOES ON.

I SAID BEFORE THAT IN THEIR OWN REALM, THE GIANTS ARE POWER-FUL.

AND ILLUSION IS THE LEAST OF THEIR POWERS.

YET WHITE-FACE'S SHARP EYES SEE WHAT OURS CANNOT.

FOR WHAT APPEARS TO BE EMPTY AIR HIDES THE **PATH** INTO JOTUNHEIM.

BALDER!

RIDE WITH ME, AGNAR! THERE IS SOLID GROUND HERE.

FORGIVE ME, BALDER, BUT I STILL PUT MORE TRUST IN THE EVIDENCE OF MY OWN SENSES THAN IN THOSE OF ANOTHER.

AND THOUGH THIS IS THE LONGER WAY, I SHALL TAKE THE SIDE ROAD HERE AND CIRCLE **AROUND** THIS TREACHEROUS ILLUSION.

THE PATH-WAY!

IT DIS-SOLVES BENEATH MY HORSE'S HOOVES!

CRUMMBLE!

MY ONLY CHANCE IS TO LEAP BACK TO THE SOLID GROUND BEFORE I, TOO, AM CARRIED TO MY DEATH IN THE CHASM BELOW.

BUT THERE IS **NO PUR-CHASE** FOR MY **FINGERS!**

MY GRIP IS **SLIP-PING!**

I CAN HOLD ON NO LONGER!

FEAR NOT, AGNAR! I HAVE YOU!

NOW DO YOU SEE WHY THE SHARP VISION OF WHITEFACE IS INVALUABLE TO US HERE?

HE SEES WHAT **NEITHER** YOU NOR I CAN SEE.

I WISH TO BE A **WARRIOR,** BALDER. I WANT **NOTHING** TO DO WITH SORCERIES!

SHOW ME AN ENEMY I CAN SEE, AN ENEMY I CAN FIGHT!

BUT THESE VERY SORCERIES **ARE** THE WEAPONS OF OUR ENEMY, AGNAR.

AND WE MUST LEARN TO FIGHT THE ENEMY NO MATTER WHAT FORM HIS ATTACK TAKES.

EVEN NOW, WHITEFACE SOARS THROUGH THE SEEMINGLY SOLID CLIFF FACE.

AND THROUGH THERE WILL I RIDE TO SAVE KARNILLA AND LEARN MORE ABOUT OUR FOES.

WILL YOU RIDE WITH ME?

THERE IS A MOMENT'S SILENCE...

...AND THEN, WITHOUT A WORD, BALDER MOUNTS AND TURNS HIS HORSE'S HEAD TOWARD THE CLIFFS.

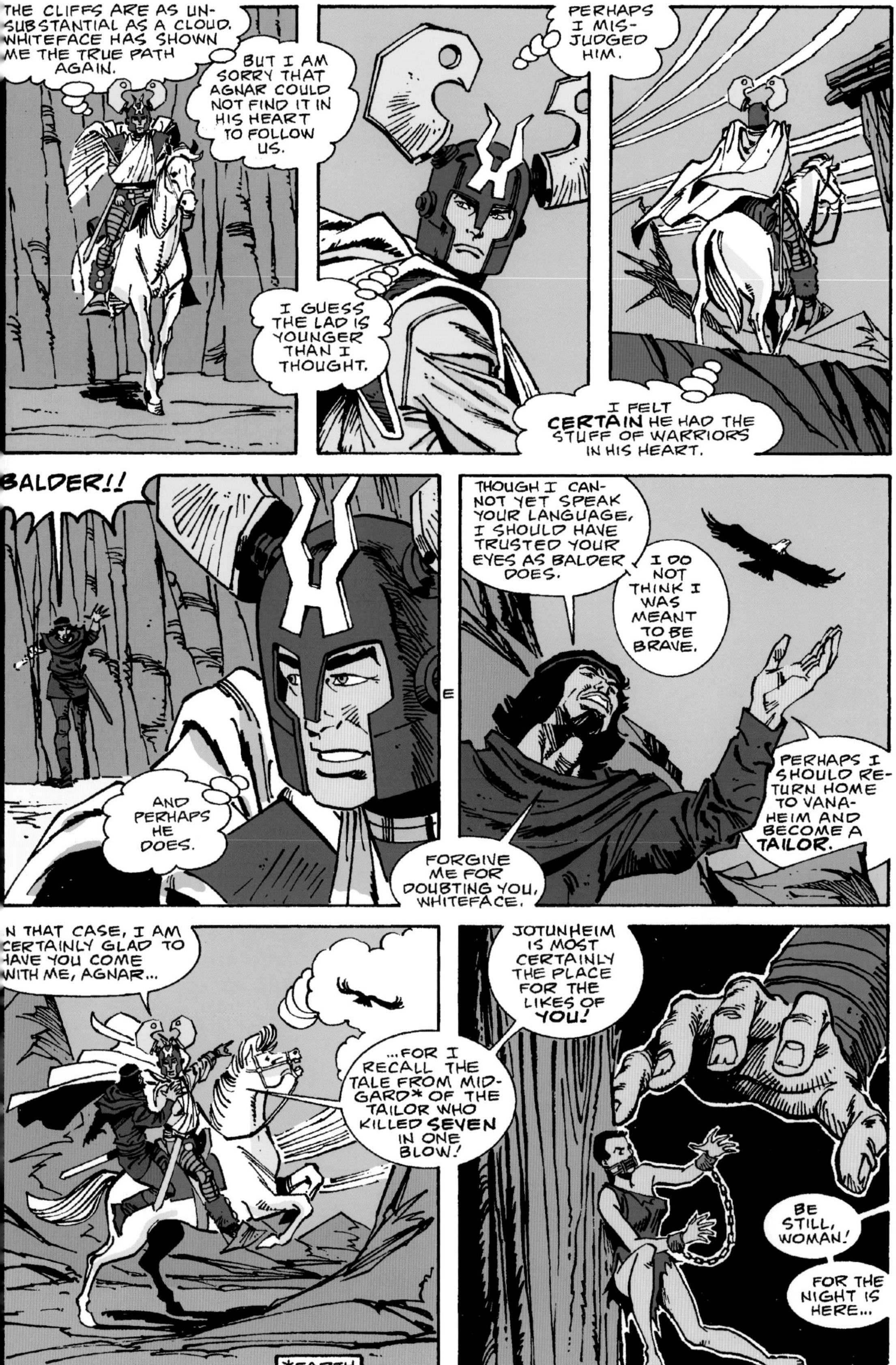
THE CLIFFS ARE AS UN-SUBSTANTIAL AS A CLOUD. WHITEFACE HAS SHOWN ME THE TRUE PATH AGAIN.
BUT I AM SORRY THAT AGNAR COULD NOT FIND IT IN HIS HEART TO FOLLOW US.
I GUESS THE LAD IS YOUNGER THAN I THOUGHT.
PERHAPS I MIS-JUDGED HIM.
I FELT CERTAIN HE HAD THE STUFF OF WARRIORS IN HIS HEART.
BALDER!!
AND PERHAPS HE DOES.
THOUGH I CAN-NOT YET SPEAK YOUR LANGUAGE, I SHOULD HAVE TRUSTED YOUR EYES AS BALDER DOES.
I DO NOT THINK I WAS MEANT TO BE BRAVE.
FORGIVE ME FOR DOUBTING YOU, WHITEFACE.
PERHAPS I SHOULD RE-TURN HOME TO VANA-HEIM AND BECOME A TAILOR.
N THAT CASE, I AM CERTAINLY GLAD TO HAVE YOU COME WITH ME, AGNAR...
...FOR I RECALL THE TALE FROM MID-GARD* OF THE TAILOR WHO KILLED SEVEN IN ONE BLOW!
*EARTH
JOTUNHEIM IS MOST CERTAINLY THE PLACE FOR THE LIKES OF YOU!
BE STILL, WOMAN!
FOR THE NIGHT IS HERE...

MY **LEGS!** HE'S **CRUSHING** THEM!

...AND NOT EVEN THE **SLAVES** OF UT-GARD-LOKI NEED WORK AFTER EVER-GLOWING HAS SET.

IN FACT, YOU HAVE DONE SO WELL TODAY THAT I SHALL **RELEASE** YOU FROM YOUR SHACKLES AND SET YOU **FREE**...

...AS FREE AS A **BIRD!**

FLY, LITTLE ONE! **FLY** BACK TO YOUR HOME...

SURELY THIS IS NOT HAPPENING!

IF I CAN BUT REACH THE WIN-DOW--!

...OR HAS THE LAND OF GIANTS SO CAPTIVATED YOUR HEART THAT YOU CANNOT BRING YOUR SELF TO LEAVE US BEHIND.

MY **WINGS** HAVE BEEN **CLIPPED!**

I AM UN ABLE T FLY!

WELL, SINCE YOU INSIST ON REMAIN-ING HERE IN JOTUN-HEIM, LITTLE DOVE...

...WE HAD BEST GIVE YOU A SAFE PLACE TO REST LEST MY CLUMSY BROTHERS STEP ON YOU THERE UPON THE FLOOR.

THERE'LL BE A FEW CRUMBS LEFT AFTER WE HAVE FEASTED.

AND NOW, BROTHERS, EAT, DRINK, AND BE MERRY...

...FOR TOMORROW, **ASGARD** SHALL SURELY FALL.

AND THE REVELRY CONTINUES LONG INTO THE NIGHT...

...THOUGH NOT ALL THE REVELERS LOSE THEMSELVES IN THE FEASTING.

STRANGE, WHAT'S THIS **UNEASE** I FEEL?

OUT THERE I SENSE THE PRESENCE OF SOMETHING GOOD, SOMETHING NOBLE...

...SOMETHING THAT DOES NOT **BELONG** IN JOTUNHEIM!

AND HIDDEN IN THE DARKNESS OF THE LAND, BENEATH A FROZEN STAND OF TREES...

...A SMALL SPARK OF WARMTH KEEPS THE COLD SHADOWS AT BAY.

THE CASTLE OF UTGARD-LOKI IS WELL-GUARDED. WE SHALL NOT GAIN ENTRANCE EASILY.

YOU ARE RIGHT. AND WE SHALL NEED ALL OUR STRENGTH.

HOW IS YOUR ARM*?

BETTER. THE LIFE IS RETURNING TO IT GRADUALLY.

*INJURED IN THOR 362!--RALF.

SNAPP!

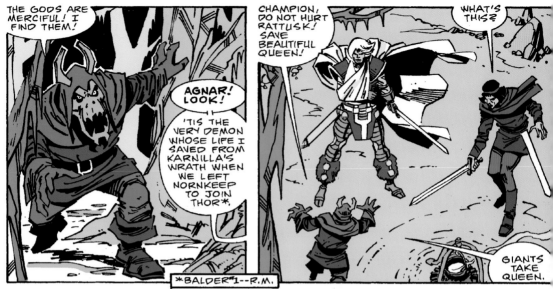

THE GODS ARE MERCIFUL! I FIND THEM!

AGNAR! LOOK!

'TIS THE VERY DEMON WHOSE LIFE I SAVED FROM KARNILLA'S WRATH WHEN WE LEFT NORNKEEP TO JOIN THOR*.

*BALDER #1--R.M.

CHAMPION, DO NOT HURT RATTUSK! SAVE BEAUTIFUL QUEEN!

WHAT'S THIS?

GIANTS TAKE QUEEN.

I ONLY ESCAPE AND FOLLOW GIANTS. BUT WHAT CAN RATTUSK DO?

THEY SO BIG, I SO SMALL.

BUT I WATCH. I CLEVER.

I FIND HIDDEN WAY INTO CASTLE. TOO SMALL FOR GIANTS... JUST RIGHT FOR RATTUSK!

NOW YOU COME FOR QUEEN... I SHOW YOU HIDDEN WAY.

VERY WELL, RATTUSK. I WILL GO WITH YOU.

SURELY, BALDER, YOU DO NOT TRUST THIS DEMON.

AND I NOT LIKE YOU, TOO.

YOU STAY! I NOT SHOW YOU HIDDEN WAY.

NOW I REALLY DO NOT TRUST HIM.

I THINK, AGNAR, THAT HE IS TELLING THE TRUTH. HE DOES KNOW A WAY INTO THE CASTLE.

AND WE BADLY NEED TO FIND A WAY IF WE ARE TO SAVE KARNILLA.

STEEP THE FIRE AND KEEP WATCH. I SHALL RETURN.

AND DO NOT WORRY.

I THINK ON THIS ADVENTURE, I SHALL FIND THE PEACE DENIED ME SINCE I LEFT HEL.

EVER SINCE WE BEGAN TO TRAVEL THE ROAD HOME, I HAVE BEEN GOADING BALDER, TRYING TO REACH HIM...

...TRYING TO GET HIM TO AWAKEN AGAIN...

...BEFORE HE SLIPPED BACK INTO THE SHELL OF APATHY THAT HAD CLAIMED HIM WHEN FIRST WE MET.

I HOPE HE IS RIGHT TO TRUST RATTUSK.

ZZZZZZ

WHAT?!!

I SAID THE HIDDEN WAY IS OPEN AND EVEN NOW RATTUSK GUARDS IT FOR US.

I HAVE RETURNED FOR YOU, BUT THE SMELL OF THE COOKING POT HAS AWAKENED MY SLEEPING STOMACH.

IS ANYTHING LEFT WITHIN?

INDEED, THERE IS.

AND IF RATTUSK MUST SHIVER IN THE COLD, 'TIS NO MORE THAN HE DESERVES, I'M SURE.

WHAT'S THIS? THE BIRDS HAVE TAKEN FLIGHT!

AND THOUGH I CANNOT SPEAK THEIR TONGUE, I CAN READ THEIR SIGNS.

THIS BEING IS NOT BALDER!

117

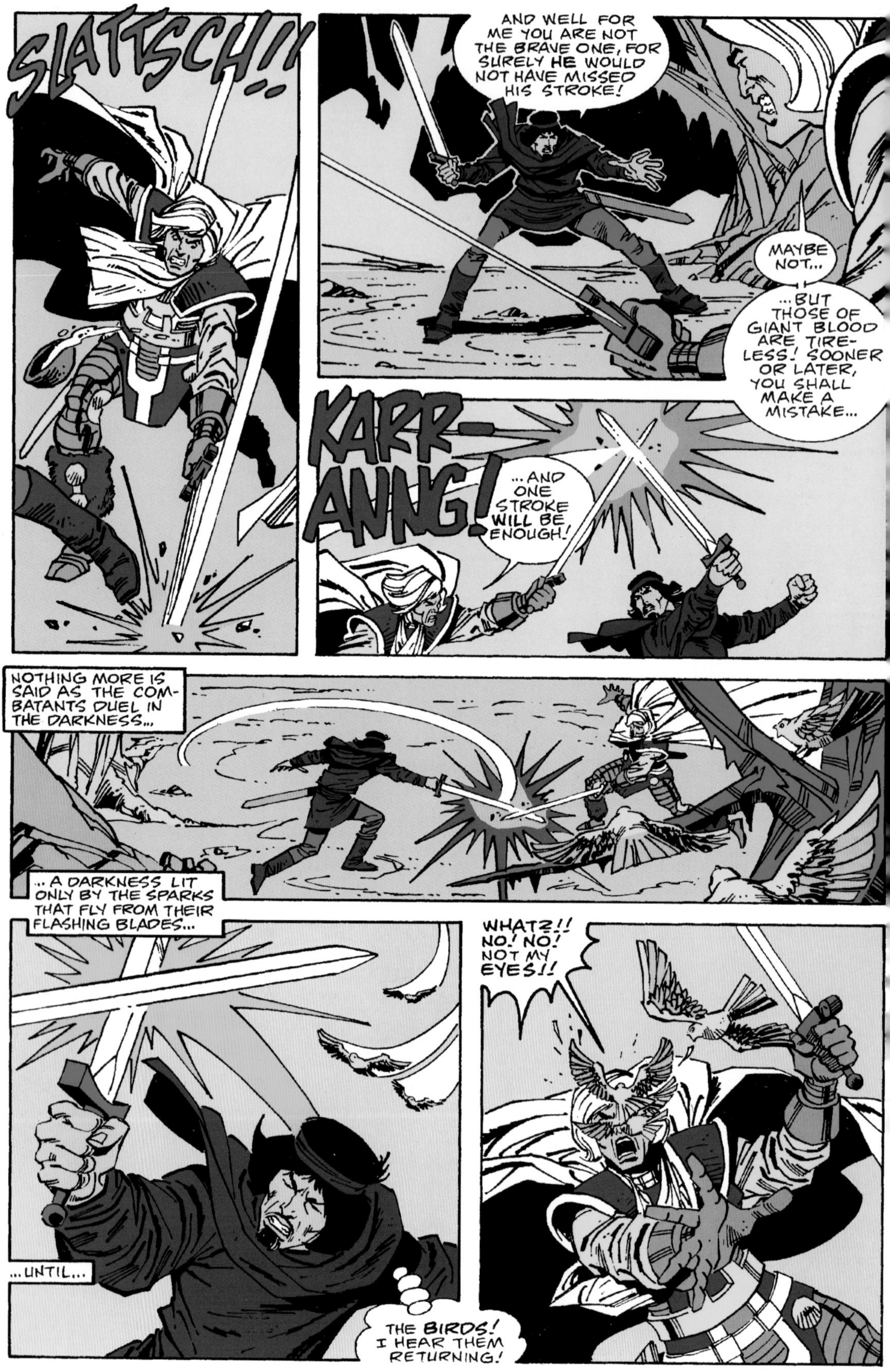
SLATTSCH!!
AND WELL FOR ME YOU ARE NOT THE BRAVE ONE, FOR SURELY HE WOULD NOT HAVE MISSED HIS STROKE!
MAYBE NOT...
...BUT THOSE OF GIANT BLOOD ARE TIRELESS! SOONER OR LATER, YOU SHALL MAKE A MISTAKE...
KARR-ANNG!
...AND ONE STROKE WILL BE ENOUGH!
NOTHING MORE IS SAID AS THE COMBATANTS DUEL IN THE DARKNESS...
...A DARKNESS LIT ONLY BY THE SPARKS THAT FLY FROM THEIR FLASHING BLADES...
...UNTIL...
THE BIRDS! I HEAR THEM RETURNING!
WHAT?!! NO! NO! NOT MY EYES!!

AND "BALDER" PROVES A TRUE PROPHET; ONE STROKE WAS INDEED ENOUGH.

GAGGGG!

AND A GENTLE HISSING FILLS THE FROZEN GLADE...

HELP ME! HELP ME! HELP ME!

WELL, LITTLE FRIEND, PERHAPS I AM FINALLY BEGINNING TO SEE AFTER ALL.

BUT WHAT OF THE *TRUE* BALDER!!

MORE THAN EVER I FEAR HE HAS FALLEN INTO A TRAP!

119

YOU **FOOL**, AGNAR, TO LET HIM GO ALONE WITH RATTUSK, NO MATTER WHAT HE SAID!

NOW SEE AS YOU WERE MEANT TO SEE AND FOLLOW THE PATH, THOUGH IT LEADS STRAIGHT INTO HELA'S WAITING ARMS!

STAND FAST, BALDER! I AM **COMING**!

THE WALLS OF THE GIANTS' FORTRESS LOOM LARGER AND LARGER...

...AND THE TREES CLOSE IN ABOUT THE PATHWAY TILL I AM BARELY ABLE TO ADVANCE ONE FOOT BEFORE THE OTHER.

IF EVER I SAW A LIKELY PLACE FOR AN **AMBUSH**, THIS IS IT.

AND AS THOUGH THE THOUGHT HAD GIVEN RISE TO THE DEED...

THERE IN THE SHADOWS OF THE PATH!

IT CAN-NOT BE!!

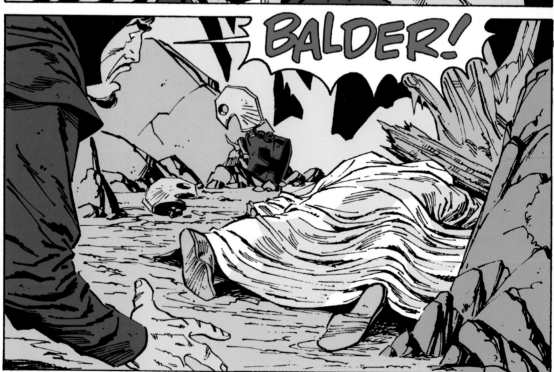

**BALDER!**

NEXT:

# BALDER:

☐ A. THE BLASTED?
☐ B. THE BLUDGEONED?
☐ C. THE BLOODY?
☐ D. THE BURIED?
☐ E. THE BYGONE?

CHECK ONE. AND DON'T MISS THE ANSWER IN THE **NEXT** EXCITING IN- STALLMENT OF... *BALDER THE BRAVE!!* ON SALE EVENTUALLY.

120

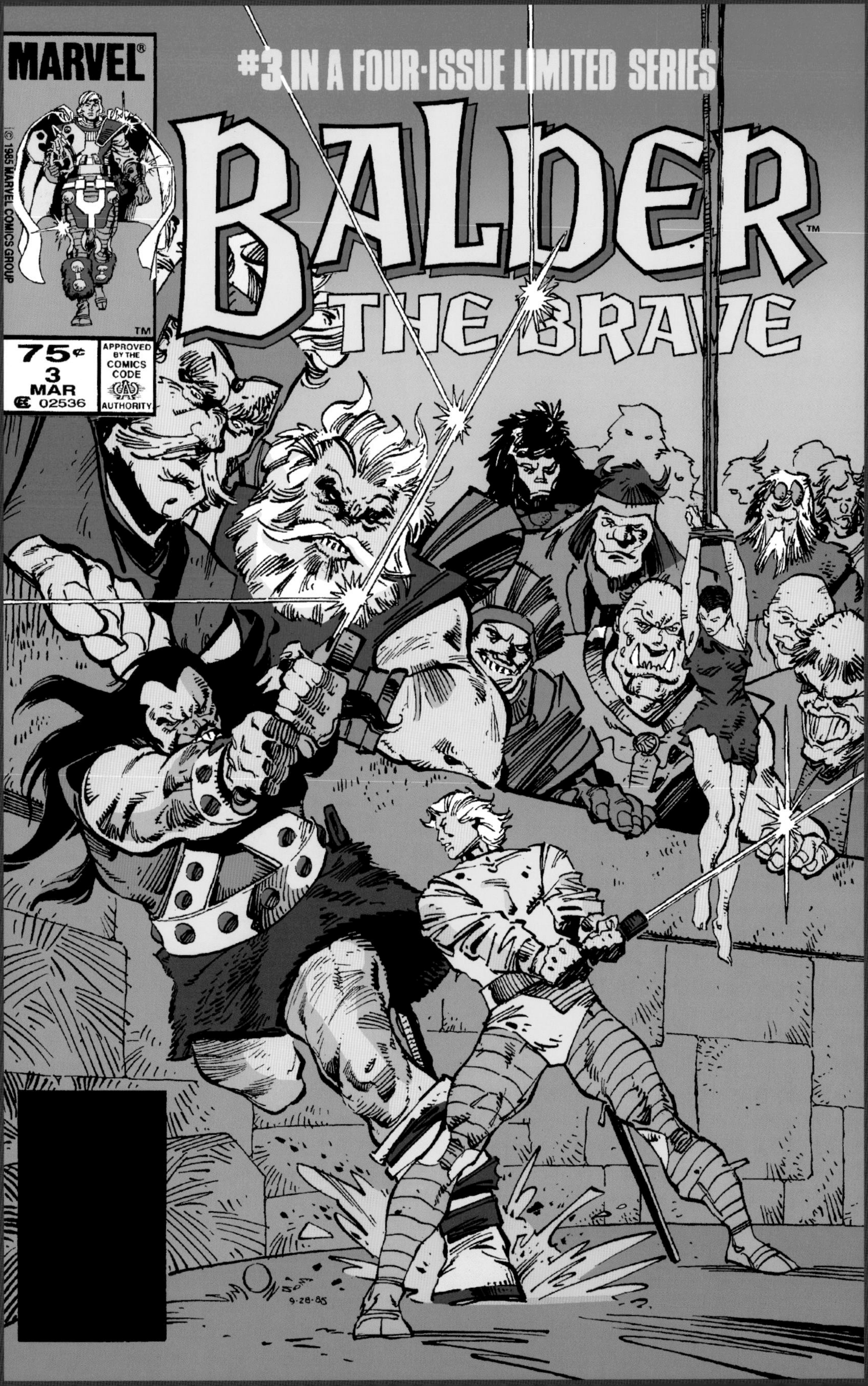
MARVEL®
© 1985 MARVEL COMICS GROUP
#3 IN A FOUR-ISSUE LIMITED SERIES
BALDER™
THE BRAVE
75¢
3
MAR
02536
APPROVED BY THE COMICS CODE AUTHORITY
9-28-85

JOTUNHEIM--WHERE WINTER'S DOMAIN ENDURES FOREVER AND SPRING IS A FORGOTTEN WORD...

JOTUNHEIM--WITHIN WHOSE ICY WASTES THE ONLY LIVING THING... IS DEATH!

BALDER! MY LORD!

WOE THAT OUR MISSION TO SAVE THE NORN QUEEN, KARNILLA, FROM THE FROST GIANTS SHOULD COME TO THIS!

BUT AGNAR SWEARS UPON THE EYE OF ODIN, BALDER, YOU SHALL BE AVENGED!

Stan Lee PRESENTS:

# Balder the WARRIOR!

WRITTEN BY
WALTER SIMONSON
ILLUSTRATED BY
SAL BUSCEMA
LETTERED BY
JOHN WORKMAN, JR.
COLORED BY
PAUL BECTON
EDITED BY
RALPH MACCHIO
EDITOR IN CHIEF:
JIM SHOOTER

I KNEW THAT WRETCHED DEMON WAS LEADING YOU INTO A TRAP*!

OH, BALDER! THOUGH I SLEW THE CHANGLING WHO WOULD HAVE SLAIN ME...

...I WAS LUCKIER THAN THEE, FOR I AM STILL ALIVE, BUT NEVER-MORE SHALL THE WORLD SEE BALDER'S LIKE AGAIN!

IF ONLY--??!!!

*DETAILS LAST ISSUE!

RATTUSK! DEAD AS A STONE! 'TIS THE VERY DEMON WHOM BALDER ACCOMPANIED!

AND WEAR-ING BALDER'S ROBES! WHAT RIDDLE IS THIS?

BEWARE, AGNAR, AND HIDE THYSELF IN THE SHADOWS! 'TIS MORE TO THIS THAN MEETS THE EYE.

YET ONLY MY EYES CAN READ THIS RIDDLE.

BEFORE ME ON THE GROUND LIES THE WRIT-ING THAT WILL TELL ME WHAT HAS BECOME OF BALDER THE BRAVE!

AND IT SHALL BE AS THOUGH AGNAR WALKED BE-SIDE HIS LORD.

NOT MUCH FURTHER, GREAT WARRIOR.

RATTUSK KNOWS THE WAY, RATTUSK HELP YOU SAVE BEAUTIFUL QUEEN!

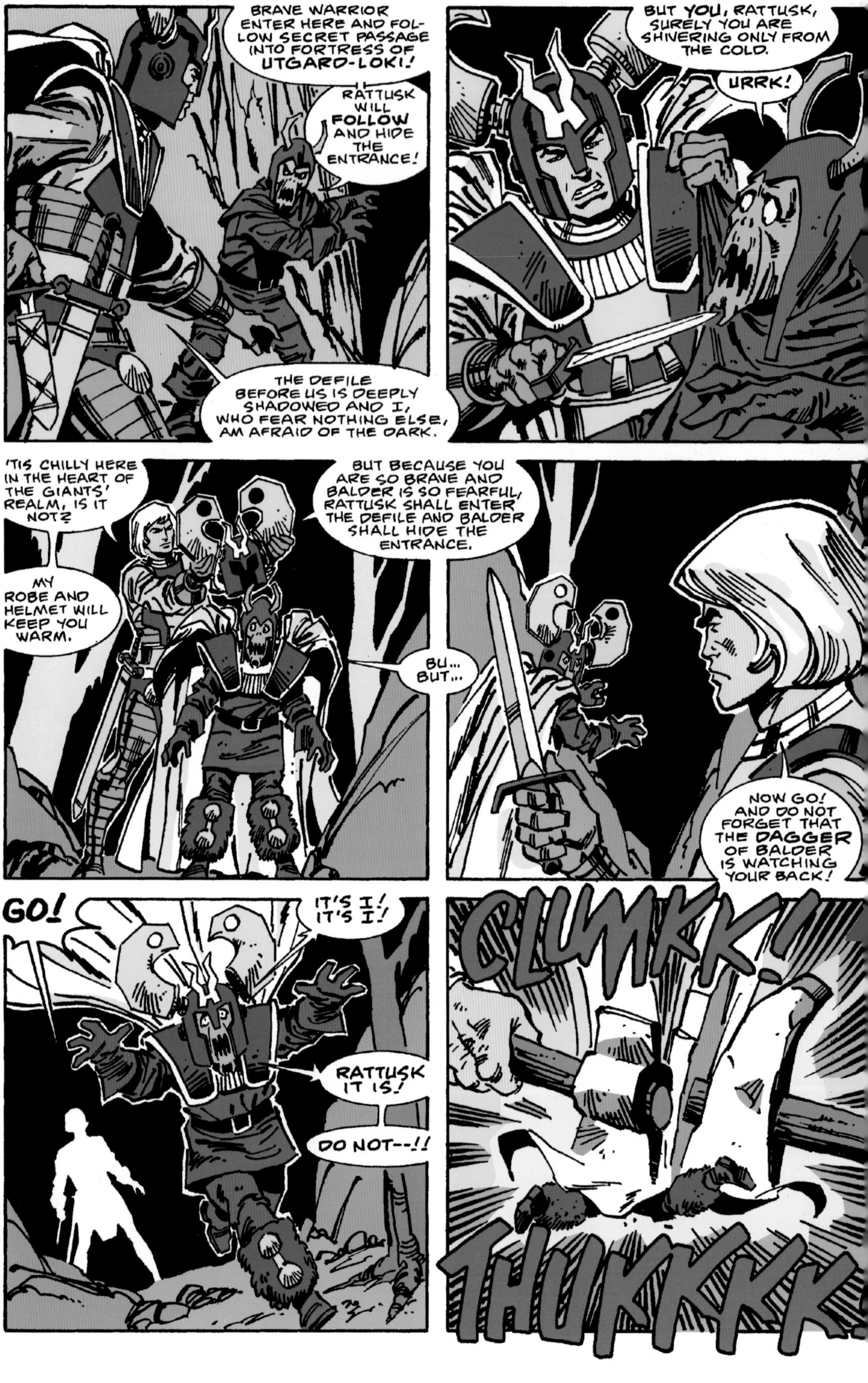
BRAVE WARRIOR ENTER HERE AND FOLLOW SECRET PASSAGE INTO FORTRESS OF UTGARD-LOKI!
RATTUSK WILL FOLLOW AND HIDE THE ENTRANCE!
THE DEFILE BEFORE US IS DEEPLY SHADOWED AND I, WHO FEAR NOTHING ELSE, AM AFRAID OF THE DARK.
BUT YOU, RATTUSK, SURELY YOU ARE SHIVERING ONLY FROM THE COLD.
URRK!
'TIS CHILLY HERE IN THE HEART OF THE GIANTS' REALM, IS IT NOT?
MY ROBE AND HELMET WILL KEEP YOU WARM.
BUT BECAUSE YOU ARE SO BRAVE AND BALDER IS SO FEARFUL, RATTUSK SHALL ENTER THE DEFILE AND BALDER SHALL HIDE THE ENTRANCE.
BU... BUT...
NOW GO! AND DO NOT FORGET THAT THE DAGGER OF BALDER IS WATCHING YOUR BACK!
GO!
IT'S I! IT'S I!
RATTUSK IT IS!
DO NOT--!!
CLUNKK!!
THUKKKK

BALDER IS **DEAD!**

**DEATH** TO THE ENEMIES OF JOTUNHEIM! DEATH TO ALL ASGARDIANS!

**HOLD!** THIS IS NOT THE BRIGHT ONE, BUT THE LITTLE DEMON WHO SWORE HE WOULD BETRAY HIM!

QUICKLY! SPREAD OUT! FIND HIM!

BALDER MUST BE HERE SOMEWHERE!

BUT AFTER A FUTILE SEARCH OF THE GROUNDS...

NO DOUBT HE'S FLED IN FEAR BEFORE OUR AWESOME WRATH!

WE MUST RETURN TO THE FORTRESS AND REPORT TO UTGARD-LOKI.

HE WON'T LIKE IT.'

AH, BUT WHAT **HARM** COULD ONE LONE GOD DO US.

AND IF THERE WERE ANY MORE ENEMIES ABOUT...

...GRUNGNIR WILL HAVE FOUND THEM AND DISPATCHED THEM BY NOW.

SO ANOTHER HAS BEEN SENT TO SLAY AGNAR.

I COULD RETURN TO HIM, BUT THIS MAY BE MY ONLY CHANCE TO ENTER THE CASTLE UNSEEN!

I CAN BUT HOPE THAT BETWEEN AGNAR AND THE BIRDS I ASKED TO WATCH OVER HIM, HE WILL BE ALL RIGHT.

I SHALL NEVER FORGIVE MYSELF IF I HAVE MADE THE WRONG CHOICE!

SO WHAT DO YOU WANT TO DO WITH THE GODS WHEN WE HAVE SACKED ASGARD?

I'LL HAVE FRIGGA TO OIL MY BEST BOOTS!

I WANT THE ENCHANTRESS TO WARM MY--!

FAUGGH! YOU BONEHEADS ARE STUPID!

I WANT IDUN'S GOLDEN APPLES! THEN I'LL LIVE FOREVER!

WELL SAID, MY BRAVE GIANT! TRULY, AMBITION DOTH RAISE HER UGLY CHILDREN IN STRANGE PLACES...

...THOUGH IF THE FATES GUIDE BALDER'S STEPS, YOU MAY ACHIEVE MUCH LESS THAN YOUR DESIRES.

BALDER'S FOOTPRINTS END ABRUPTLY HERE BEHIND THOSE OF ONE OF THE GIANTS.

SO EVEN NOW, BALDER MUST BE WITHIN THE FORTRESS OF UTGARD-LOKI, LORD OF THE FROST GIANTS OF JOTUNHEIM AND OUR BITTER ENEMY.

HO, WITHIN! OPEN THE PORTAL!

WE HAVE RETURNED.

COME, WE MUST MAKE HASTE TO THE COUNCIL ROOM.

THEN PERHAPS BALDER SHOULD MAKE HASTE IN SOME OTHER DIRECTION.

YET ALREADY I KNOW SOMETHING OF WHICH NO OTHER ASGARDIAN IS AWARE.

THE DESTRUCTION OF KARNILLA'S KINGDOM WAS THE BEGINNING OF AN ORCHESTRATED CAMPAIGN TO DESTROY ASGARD AND HER ALLIES!

AND UTGARD-LOKI IS BEHIND IT ALL.

I MUST RETURN TO ASGARD TO WARN THOR AND THE REST OF THE GOLDEN REALM!

EVEN KARNILLA'S LIFE MAY NOT BE WORTH THE COST OF THIS INFORMATION IF ASGARD FAILS TO LEARN OF HER DANGER IN TIME!

BUT I CANNOT LEAVE JOTUNHEIM WITHOUT LEARN-ING, IF I CAN, WHAT HAS BE-COME OF HER.

I SHALL ALLOW MY-SELF A FEW MOMENTS ONLY TO SCOUT THE GIANT-HOLD...

...IN ORDER TO LEARN THEIR STRENGTHS AND PLANS.

BUT IF I CAN FIND NO TRACE OF KARNILLA, I SHALL HAVE TO ABANDON HER HERE.

BY THE SPIRES OF ASGARD, THE COLD OF THIS CASTLE WOULD CHILL THE BLOOD OF THE WARMEST GOD!

SURELY 'TIS EVEN COLDER WITHIN THAN WITHOUT.

WHAT HAVE WE HERE?

127

A HARMLESS SPARROW, CAUGHT NO DOUBT BY THE GIANTS AND HUNG IN THIS FRIGID CHAMBER FOR THEIR SADISTIC AMUSEMENT.

THE HALL IS EMPTY AND IT WILL BE BUT THE WORK OF A MOMENT...

...TO REACH THE CAGE...

...AND FREE ITS OCCUPANT!

WOULD THAT I COULD FIND KARNILLA AS EASILY!

FLY, LITTLE ONE. FLY TO FREEDOM FROM THESE DREARY HALLS OF ICE.

IT FLUTTERS TO THE GROUND, UNABLE TO GAIN THE AIR!

POOR CREATURE, NOT CONTENT TO CAGE YOU, THE GIANTS HAVE CLIPPED YOUR WINGS AS WELL.

AND YOU CANNOT SPEAK, EITHER.

THE LANGUAGE OF THE BIRDS IS NO MYSTERY TO ME, BUT I DO NOT UNDERSTAND YOUR CRIES, MUCH AS YOU SEEM TO WISH ME TO.

CHEEP CHEEP

ANOTHER CRUELTY OF THE GIANTS, PERHAPS.

FEAR NOT, LITTLE ONE.

YOU SHALL COME WITH BALDER.

...AND WHEN HE HAS LEFT JOTUNHEIM FAR BEHIND...

...THE FREEDOM OF THE SKIES OF THE GOLDEN REALM SHALL BE THINE.

BUT TILL THAT MOMENT, WE SHALL EXPLORE THE GIANT HOLD TOGETHER.

I SEARCH FOR MY HEART.

ONE AFTER ANOTHER, THE HALLS OF UTGARD-LOKI ARE EMPTY.

SURELY HE HAS NOT YET GATHERED ALL HIS MINIONS TOGETHER TO ATTACK ASGARD SO SOON.

BUT THE AIR GROWS COLDER AND COLDER BY THE MINUTE AND EVEN MY LIMBS BEGIN TO STIFFEN.

LITTLE FRIEND!

THIS INNOCENT BIRD IS FREEZING TO DEATH BEFORE MY VERY EYES.

AND THERE IS NAUGHT I CAN DO TO PREVENT IT!

129

WAIT! WHAT IS THIS? THE SPARROW BEGINS TO FLUTTER WITH NEW LIFE IN MY HANDS!

I AM RADIATING BOTH LIGHT AND HEAT AS THOUGH I WERE THE SUN ITSELF!

I FEEL AS THOUGH I COULD GLOW LIKE THE SUN SIMPLY BY WILLING IT TO HAPPEN.

AND THE ARM THAT HELA WOUNDED* IS FILLED AGAIN WITH LIFE!

AND MY HANDS ARE BEGINNING TO GLOW! LIFE-GIVING WARMTH SUFFUSES MY ENTIRE BODY!

*THAT WAS IN THOR 361 IF YOU MISSED IT! AND SHAME ON YOU, TOO!

NEVER BEFORE HAVE I FELT SO STRONG, SO CERTAIN OF MY OWN PROWESS.

SURELY, THIS IS SOME AFTER-EFFECT OF THE TRAINING PROGRAM I UNDERTOOK WITH AGNAR...

...WHEN FIRST WE DECIDED TO FOLLOW THO INTO HEL*.

*BALDER THE BRAVE 1

AND AS YOU REVIVE, LITTLE ONE, SO MY HOPES TO FIND KARNILLA REVIVE AS WELL.

IF I CANNOT ABANDON YOU, HOW CAN I ABANDON THE NORN QUEEN, THOUGH ALL OF ASGARD SHOULD HANG IN THE BALANCE?

MUST I MEASURE THE LIVES OF MY BEST COMPANIONS AND MY COUNTRY AGAINST THE LIFE OF THE WOMAN I LOVE...

...I WHO HAVE LOST ONE LOVE ALREADY TO THE ICY GRIP OF DEATH*?

*THOR 361 AGAIN!

130

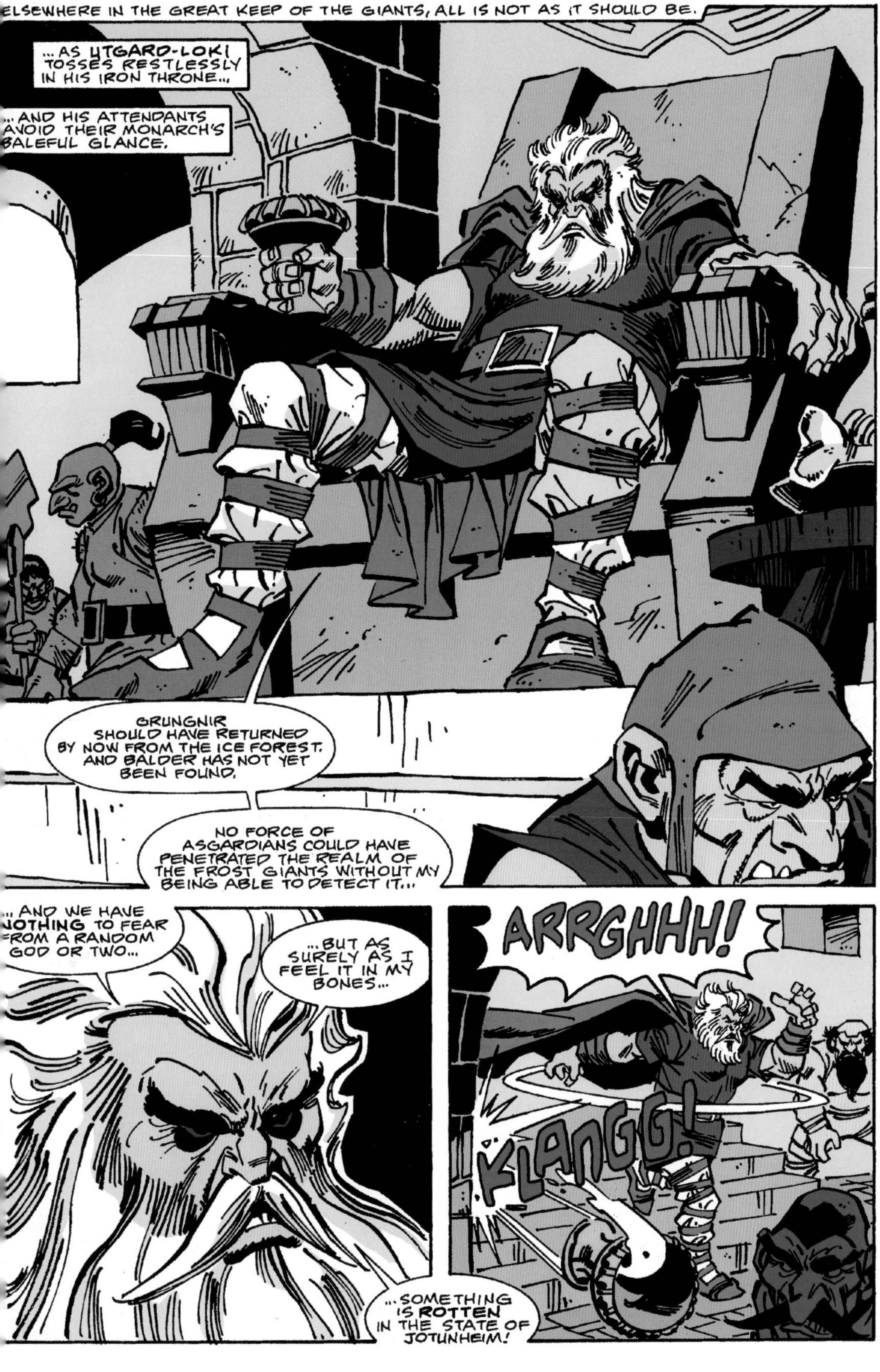
ELSEWHERE IN THE GREAT KEEP OF THE GIANTS, ALL IS NOT AS IT SHOULD BE.
...AS UTGARD-LOKI TOSSES RESTLESSLY IN HIS IRON THRONE...
...AND HIS ATTENDANTS AVOID THEIR MONARCH'S BALEFUL GLANCE.
GRUNGNIR SHOULD HAVE RETURNED BY NOW FROM THE ICE FOREST. AND BALDER HAS NOT YET BEEN FOUND.
NO FORCE OF ASGARDIANS COULD HAVE PENETRATED THE REALM OF THE FROST GIANTS WITHOUT MY BEING ABLE TO DETECT IT...
...AND WE HAVE NOTHING TO FEAR FROM A RANDOM GOD OR TWO...
...BUT AS SURELY AS I FEEL IT IN MY BONES...
ARRGHHH!
KLANGG!
...SOMETHING IS ROTTEN IN THE STATE OF JOTUNHEIM!

YOU TWO COME WITH ME. WE GO TO CHECK ON OUR UNWILLING GUEST, KARNILLA.

PERHAPS SHE HAS SOMETHING TO DO WITH THIS UNEASE I FEEL!

AND IF SHE DOES, HEAVILY SHALL SHE PAY FOR IT!

WAIT!

WHAT DO I FEEL IN YONDER HALLWAY?

WARMTH? IN THE CASTLE OF UTGARD-LOKI?

ATTEND ME! AND MOVE AS SILENTLY AS THOUGH YOU HAD THE GRACE OF FAERIES OR RISK MY DISPLEASURE!

SOMETHING THERE IS HERE THAT DOES NOT LOVE THE FROST GIANTS!

WHILE NOT FAR AWAY...

WE ARE WARM ENOUGH NOW, MY LITTLE FRIEND.

BUT NO MATTER WHAT THE PERIL TO ASGARD, I CANNOT LEAVE TILL I KNOW WHAT HAS BECOME OF KARNILLA.

THOUGH DANGER LURKS IN EVERY CORNER, WE WILL SEARCH THE REST OF UTGARD-LOKI'S KEEP!

CHEEP! CHEEP! CHEEP!

WHAT?!!

132

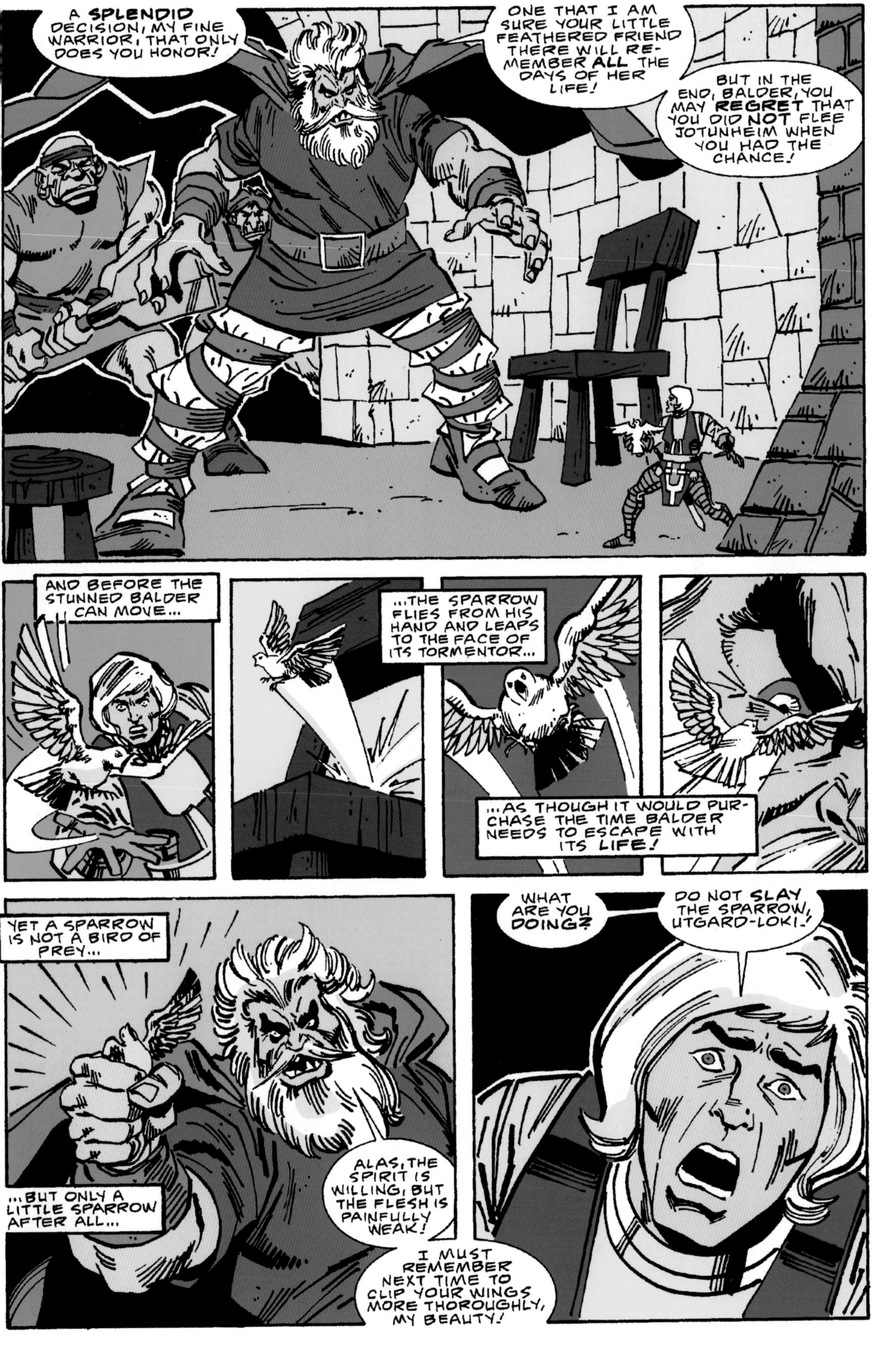
A SPLENDID DECISION, MY FINE WARRIOR, THAT ONLY DOES YOU HONOR!
ONE THAT I AM SURE YOUR LITTLE FEATHERED FRIEND THERE WILL REMEMBER ALL THE DAYS OF HER LIFE!
BUT IN THE END, BALDER, YOU MAY REGRET THAT YOU DID NOT FLEE JOTUNHEIM WHEN YOU HAD THE CHANCE!
AND BEFORE THE STUNNED BALDER CAN MOVE...
...THE SPARROW FLIES FROM HIS HAND AND LEAPS TO THE FACE OF ITS TORMENTOR...
...AS THOUGH IT WOULD PURCHASE THE TIME BALDER NEEDS TO ESCAPE WITH ITS LIFE!
YET A SPARROW IS NOT A BIRD OF PREY...
...BUT ONLY A LITTLE SPARROW AFTER ALL...
ALAS, THE SPIRIT IS WILLING, BUT THE FLESH IS PAINFULLY WEAK!
I MUST REMEMBER NEXT TIME TO CLIP YOUR WINGS MORE THOROUGHLY, MY BEAUTY!
WHAT ARE YOU DOING?
DO NOT SLAY THE SPARROW, UTGARD-LOKI!

HAVE NO FEAR OF THAT, BALDER. AT LEAST, NOT YET.

WERE I TO SLAY THE SPARROW NOW, I WOULD DEPRIVE MY-SELF OF A CHARMING GUEST...

...AND LOSE THE HOLD I ALREADY HAVE OVER BALDER THE BRAVE, THE NOBLEST WARRIOR OF ASGARD.

THE ILLUSIONS OF UTGARD-LOKI ARE TRULY WITH-OUT PEER, ARE THEY NOT, BALDER?

KARNILLA!

INDEED!

WELCOME, BALDER, TO THE HOUSE OF THE FROST GIANTS.

SINCE YOU HAVE COME SO FAR TO SEE OUR GUEST, WE MUST ARRANGE A SUITABLE ENTERTAINMENT.

WHY NOT JOIN KARNILLA AND MYSELF IN THE GREAT HALL AND WE SHALL SEE IF WE CANNOT AMUSE OURSELVES THIS EVENING.

WE SHALL SUMMON HAGEN TO THE HALL. HE IS MORE THE SCALE OF OUR LATEST VISITOR, IS HE NOT, LADS?

AND THE REALM OF UTGARD-LOKI IS FILLED WITH GIGANTIC LAUGHTER!

MEANWHILE, OUTSIDE THE FORTRESS...

STRANGE. THE GROUND DOTH QUIVER GENTLY BENEATH MY FEET.

AVOIDING THE GIANTS WHO STILL SEARCH THE GROUNDS HAS BEEN CHILD'S PLAY...

BUT I AM NO CLOSER TO EFFECTING AN ENTRANCE INTO THE CASTLE OF UTGARD-LOKI THAN I WAS WHEN I LEFT RATTUSK'S BODY.

AND BALDER MAY BE IN DIRE NEED OF HELP.

WHITEFACE! LORD OF EAGLES!

AND ANXIOUS TO SHOW ME SOMETHING, I'LL WARRANT.

LEAD ON AND I WILL FOLLOW.

CURSE THE FACT THAT I HAVE NOT LEARNED TO SPEAK THE LANGUAGE OF THE BIRDS.

IF WE SURVIVE THIS ADVENTURE, THE FIRST THING I SHALL DO UPON MY RETURN HOME IS PERSUADE BALDER TO TEACH ME FLUENT AVIAN.

I HAVE ALWAYS HATED CHARADES!

BUT SEE WHAT WHITEFACE HAS FOUND, HIDDEN DEEP WITHIN THE SHADOWS OF THE FURTHEST CASTLE WALL.

AN UN-BARRED WINDOW, NOT A HUNDRED FEET ABOVE THE GROUND

AND AN ICY FACING BELOW IT THAT I MAY YET BE ABLE TO ASCEND!

THANK YOU, WHITE-FACE. AT ANOTHER TIME, PERHAPS, I WILL BE ABLE TO REWARD YOU SUITABLE FOR THIS SERVICE.

ASSUMING THAT I LIVE LONG ENOUGH TO BE ABLE TO REWARD ANY BUT MY UNDER-TAKER.

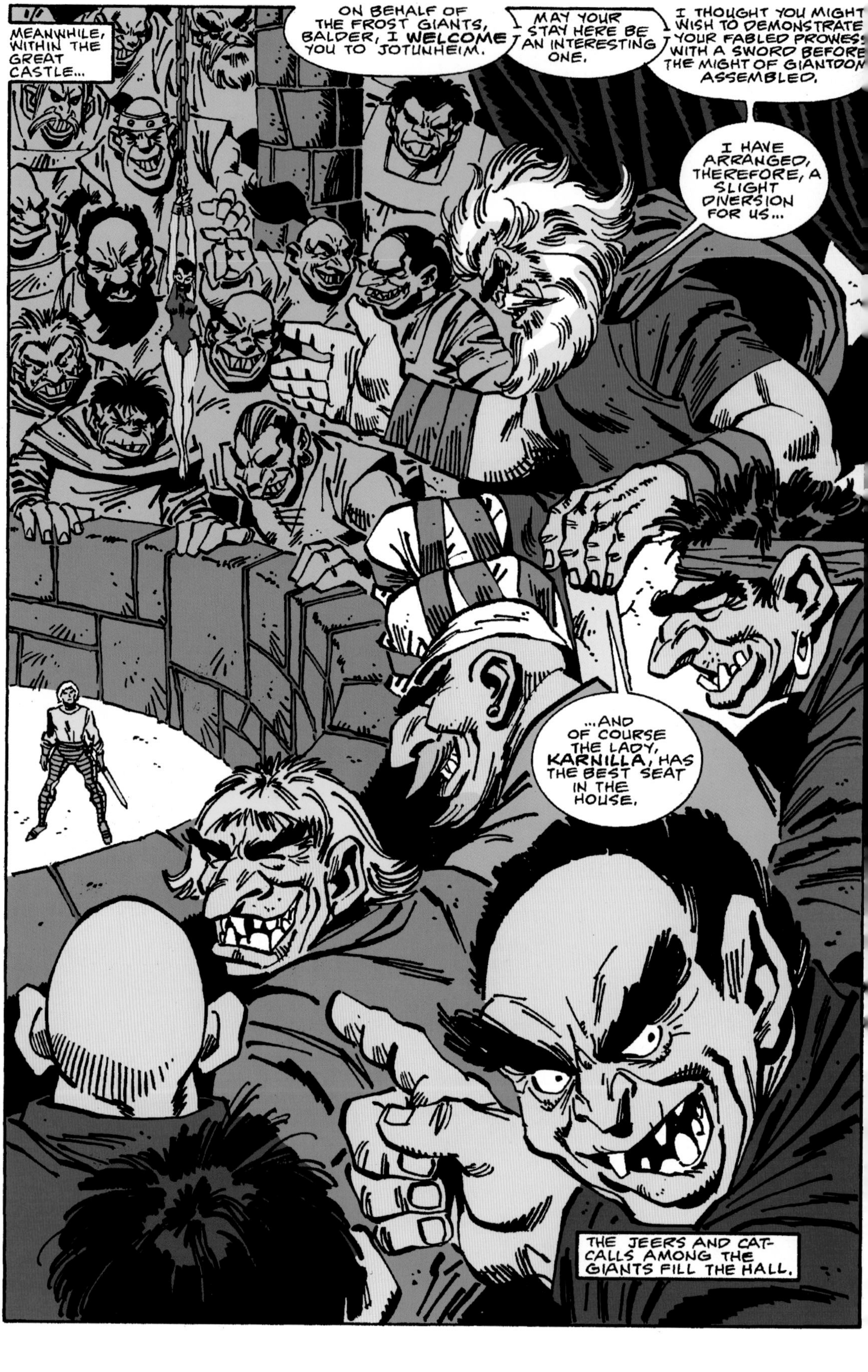
MEANWHILE, WITHIN THE GREAT CASTLE...
ON BEHALF OF THE FROST GIANTS, BALDER, I WELCOME YOU TO JOTUNHEIM.
MAY YOUR STAY HERE BE AN INTERESTING ONE.
I THOUGHT YOU MIGHT WISH TO DEMONSTRATE YOUR FABLED PROWESS WITH A SWORD BEFORE THE MIGHT OF GIANTDOM ASSEMBLED.
I HAVE ARRANGED, THEREFORE, A SLIGHT DIVERSION FOR US...
...AND OF COURSE THE LADY, KARNILLA, HAS THE BEST SEAT IN THE HOUSE.
THE JEERS AND CAT-CALLS AMONG THE GIANTS FILL THE HALL.

NATURALLY, NO GIANT WOULD WISH TO DEMEAN HIS HONOR DEFEATING SUCH A *SMALL FOE* AS YOURSELF...

...THOUGH NATURALLY, HE IS ONLY A *LITTLE* GIANT AND SHOULD BE AN EASY MATCH FOR ONE OF YOUR ABILITIES...

...SO WE HAVE PROVIDED A MORE SUITABLY *SCALED* OPPONENT.

ALLOW ME, *LITTLE GOD,* TO INTRODUCE *HAGEN OF TRONOGARRO,* AN *INCOMPARABLE* SWORDSMAN.

HE SEEKS TO *LULL* ME WITH WORDS WHEN BEFORE ME I SEE ONE OF THE *DEADLIEST WEAPONS* IN ALL THE NINE WORLDS!

SURELY HAGEN WIELDS NOTHING LESS THAN THE *LONG LOST SWORD OF FREY,* THE BLADE THAT FIGHTS BY *ITSELF...* AND CUTS THROUGH *ANY DEFENSE!*

SUCH A WEAPON IN THE HANDS OF A *MASTER* WOULD MAKE AN *INVINCIBLE SWORDSMAN!*

TO FACE THE *SWORD OF FREY* IS TO *DIE;* TO ATTEMPT TO ESCAPE WITHOUT A FIGHT IS TO *DOOM KARNILLA!*

137

HAGEN MOVES WITH THE GRACE AND SKILL OF A BORN SWORDS-MAN!

EVEN WITHOUT THE SWORD OF FREY, THERE WOULD BE NO WEAKNESS IN HIS DEFENSE.

WITHOUT DOUBT, MY LIFE SPAN CAN ONLY BE MEASURED IN SECONDS!

AND THAT THOUGHT HAS OCCURRED TO ANOTHER AS WELL!

YOU ARE ABOUT TO WITNESS A SIGHT WE GIANTS HAVE LONGED TO SEE FOR, LO, THESE ENDLESS MILLENNIA...

WILL YOU NOT OPEN YOUR EYES, KARNILLA?

...WHEN THE GODS BOW DOWN AND GIANTS WALK THE EARTH!

THE CROWD BEHIND HIM SHRIEKS FOR MY BLOOD, BUT HAGEN ATTACKS WITHOUT A WORD!

THOUGH HE WIELDS THE SWORD INVINCIBLE, STILL HE MOVES WARILY...

...RESPECT-ING HIS OPPONENT.

AND THAT MEANS I HAVE VIRTUALLY NO CHANCE OF MOVING INSIDE HIS GUARD EVEN IF HE WERE NOT PROTECTED BY THE MAGIC SWORD!

HAGEN'S SPEED IS UNBELIEVABLE!

ONLY MY GREAT AGILITY HAS KEPT ME FROM BEING SPLITTED UPON HIS BLADE ALREADY...

...BUT THIS IS JUST A DELAYING ACTION!

SOONER OR LATER, I SHALL TIRE AND COMMIT A MISTAKE...

...WHEREAS THE SWORD OF FREY WILL NEVER ERR.

AND THAT MEANS THAT SOONER OR LATER, NO MATTER WHAT, I SHALL DIE!

138

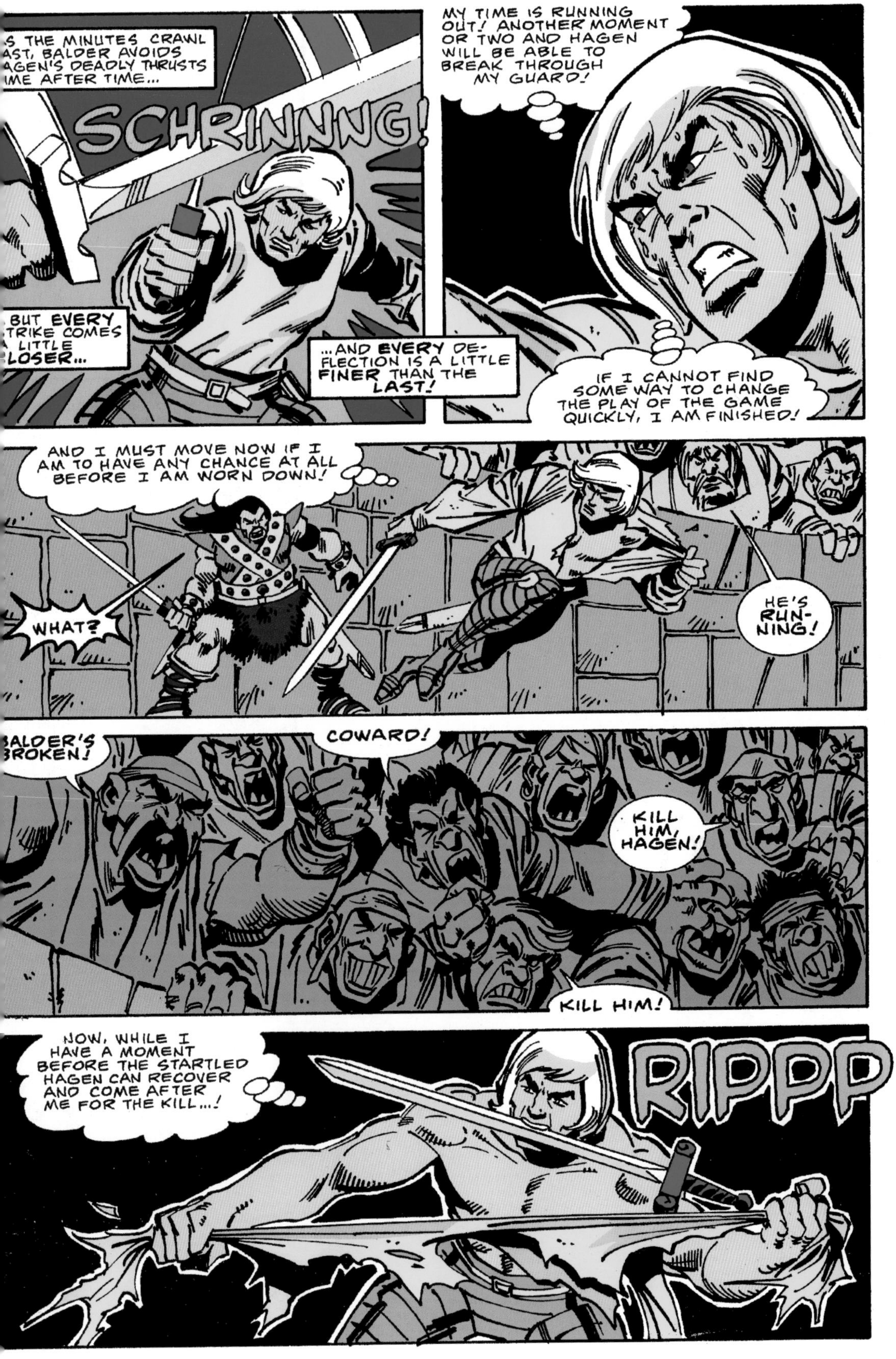
...S THE MINUTES CRAWL ...AST, BALDER AVOIDS ...AGEN'S DEADLY THRUSTS ...IME AFTER TIME...
SCHRINNNG!
...BUT EVERY ...TRIKE COMES ... LITTLE ...LOSER...
...AND EVERY DEFLECTION IS A LITTLE FINER THAN THE LAST!
MY TIME IS RUNNING OUT! ANOTHER MOMENT OR TWO AND HAGEN WILL BE ABLE TO BREAK THROUGH MY GUARD!
IF I CANNOT FIND SOME WAY TO CHANGE THE PLAY OF THE GAME QUICKLY, I AM FINISHED!
AND I MUST MOVE NOW IF I AM TO HAVE ANY CHANCE AT ALL BEFORE I AM WORN DOWN!
WHAT?
HE'S RUNNING!
...ALDER'S ...ROKEN!
COWARD!
KILL HIM, HAGEN!
KILL HIM!
NOW, WHILE I HAVE A MOMENT BEFORE THE STARTLED HAGEN CAN RECOVER AND COME AFTER ME FOR THE KILL...!
RIPPP

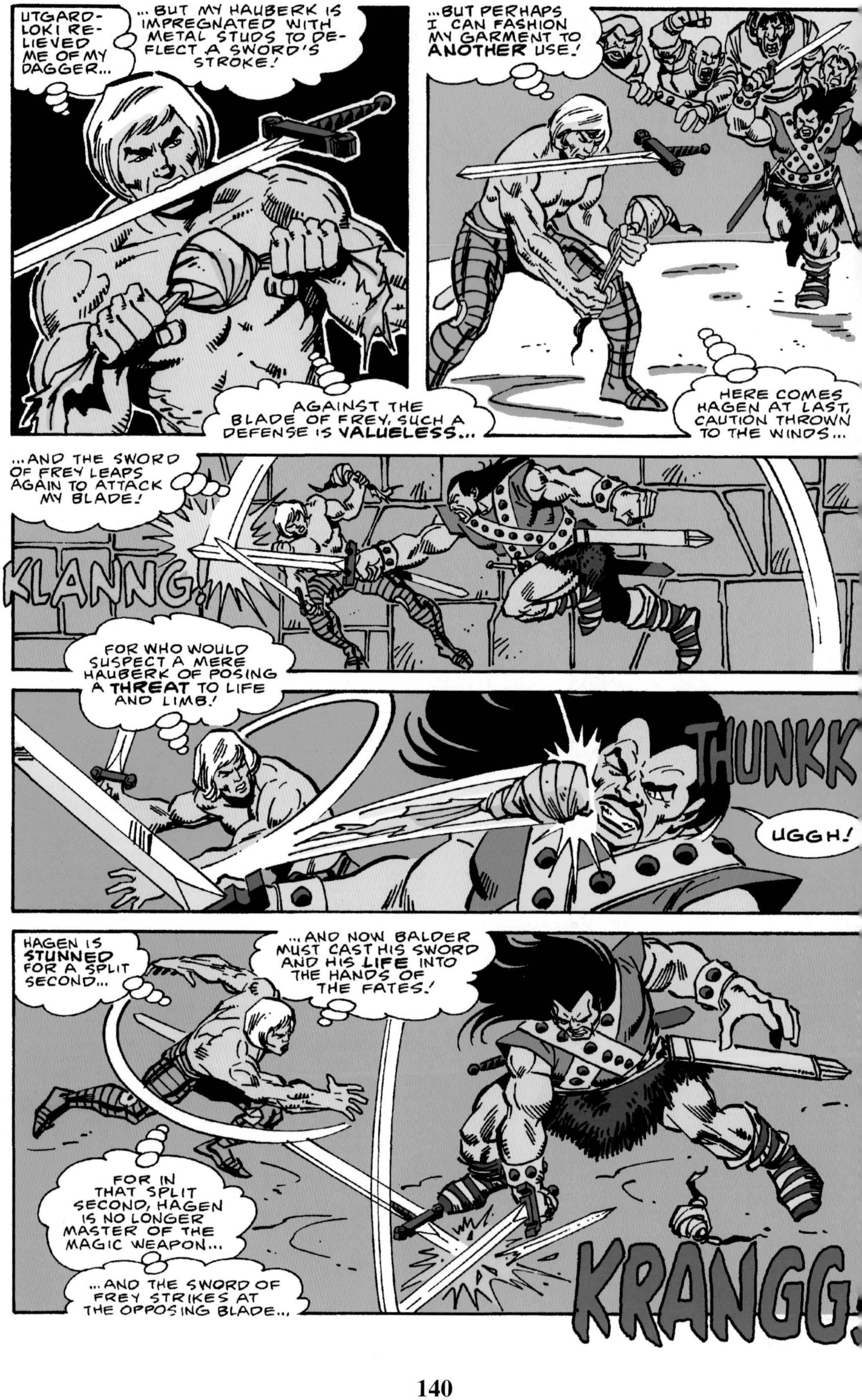

UTGARD-LOKI RELIEVED ME OF MY DAGGER...
...BUT MY HAUBERK IS IMPREGNATED WITH METAL STUDS TO DEFLECT A SWORD'S STROKE!
AGAINST THE BLADE OF FREY, SUCH A DEFENSE IS VALUELESS...
...BUT PERHAPS I CAN FASHION MY GARMENT TO ANOTHER USE!
HERE COMES HAGEN AT LAST, CAUTION THROWN TO THE WINDS...
...AND THE SWORD OF FREY LEAPS AGAIN TO ATTACK MY BLADE!
KLANNG!
FOR WHO WOULD SUSPECT A MERE HAUBERK OF POSING A THREAT TO LIFE AND LIMB!
THUNKK
UGGH!
HAGEN IS STUNNED FOR A SPLIT SECOND...
...AND NOW BALDER MUST CAST HIS SWORD AND HIS LIFE INTO THE HANDS OF THE FATES!
FOR IN THAT SPLIT SECOND, HAGEN IS NO LONGER MASTER OF THE MAGIC WEAPON...
...AND THE SWORD OF FREY STRIKES AT THE OPPOSING BLADE...
KRANGG

...LEAVING AN OPENING WITHIN ITS DEADLY ARC WHEREIN I MAY GRAPPLE MY ENEMY. HAND TO HAND!

WELL DONE, LITTLE GOD!

BUT DESPITE HIS SIZE, HAGEN IS A GIANT AND NO GOD CAN OVERCOME HIM BY MATCHING STRENGTH WITH STRENGTH!

IN A MOMENT, I... WILL FREE MY SWORD ARM AND WHEN I DO... WEAPONLESS BALDER SHALL ...DIE!!

BRAG-GART! THE GODS WERE EVER MASTERS OF THE GIANTS!

JUST ASK THOR THE NEXT TIME HE FARES FORTH TO JOTUNHEIM AND UTGARD-LOKI FEARS AGAIN TO FACE HIM AS HE DID IN THE PAST *!

*A TALE FROM THE MYTHS THAT WE MAY ONE DAY RELATE!

BUT THE HANDS OF BALDER ARE THE HANDS OF THE SUN...

...AND FOR ALL YOUR PROWESS, HAGEN, YOU ARE A FROST GIANT!

ARRRGH! MY WRIST!

SSSSHSSSS!

I CAN NO LONGER GRIP THE BLADE!

THEN HAGEN IS NO LONGER WIELDER OF THE MAGIC SWORD!

TREACH-EROUS LITTLE WORM!

HAGEN IS A TWO-HANDED MASTER OF ANY BLADE!

HE DOES NOT NEED THE SWORD OF FREY TO SLAY HIS ENEMIES!

YOU ARE A MASTER WITH A SWORD, HAGEN...

SHRIINGG!

...BUT BALDER IS THE MASTER OF MANY FORMS OF COMBAT...

...AND THIS COMBAT IS YOUR LAST.!!

SCHRAKKK

FOR A MOMENT, THERE IS ONLY STUNNED SILENCE IN THE HALLS OF UTGARD-LOKI...

...AND IN THE MOMENT, BALDER RECOVERS WHAT THE GODS HAD ONCE LOST!

BALDER! MY LORD! LOOK ABOVE YOU!

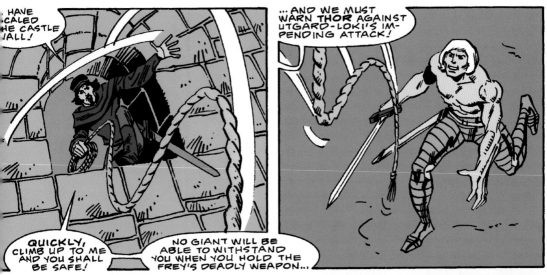

...AND WE MUST WARN **THOR** AGAINST UTGARD-LOKI'S IMPENDING ATTACK!

HAVE SCALED THE CASTLE WALL!

QUICKLY, CLIMB UP TO ME AND YOU SHALL BE SAFE!

NO GIANT WILL BE ABLE TO WITHSTAND YOU WHEN YOU HOLD THE FREY'S DEADLY WEAPON...

NOT SO FAST, YOU SCUM OF ASGARD!

HAVE YOU **FORGOTTEN** SO QUICKLY THAT I HOLD THE **LIFE** OF THE **NORN QUEEN** IN MY VERY HAND?

THROW DOWN YOUR WEAPONS, BOTH OF YOU, AND **SURRENDER** TO THE FROST GIANTS...

...OR **KARNILLA** DIES HERE AND NOW!!

# DON'T MISS

BALDER THE BRAVE, PART FOUR, **BALDER THE BEAUTIFUL!** WHERE THINGS DO NOT END HAPPILY EVER AFTER!

(AFTER ALL, WE DON'T WANT TO WRITE OURSELVES OUT OF A JOB!)

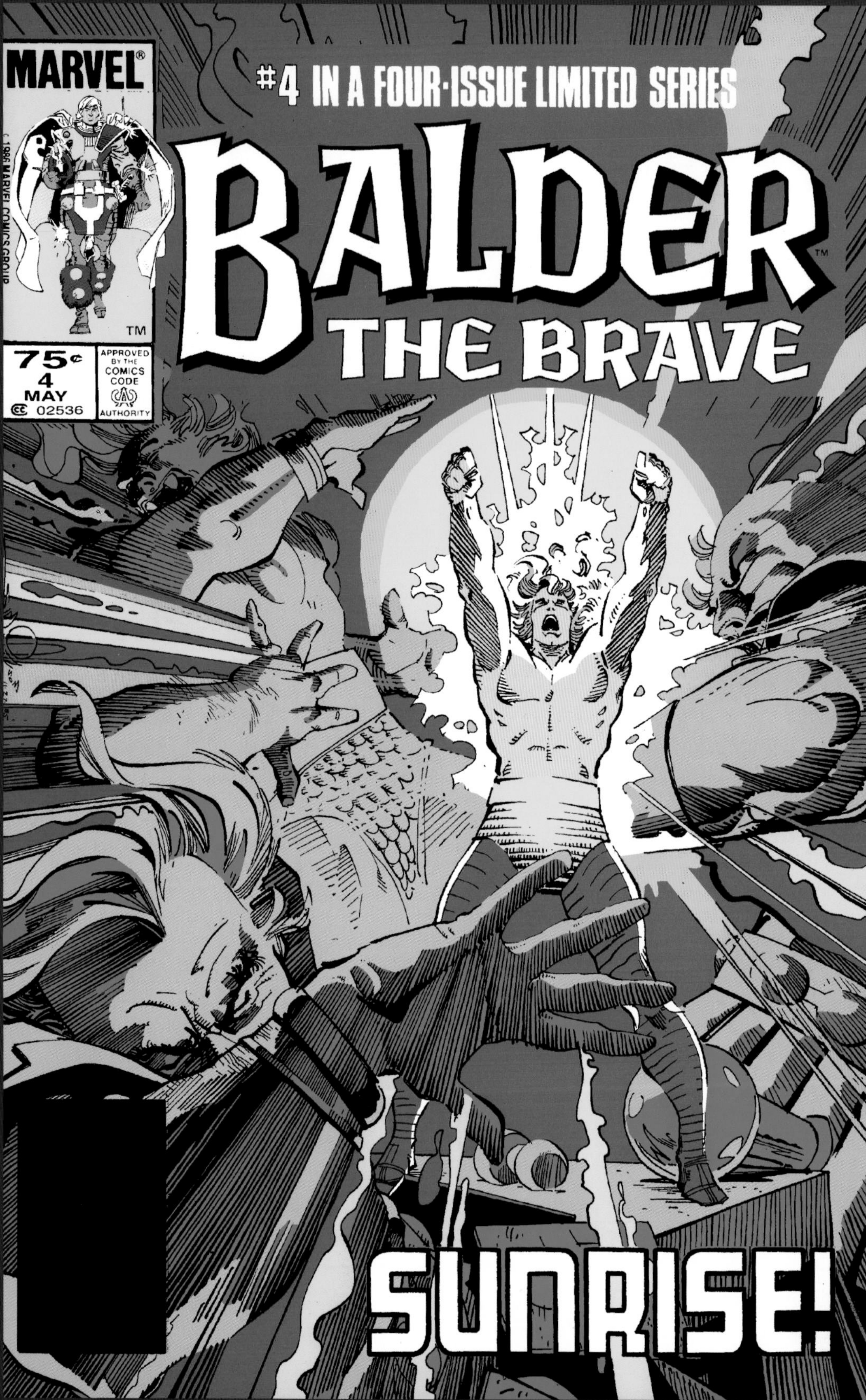
MARVEL®
#4 IN A FOUR-ISSUE LIMITED SERIES
BALDER™
THE BRAVE
TM
75¢
4
MAY
02536
APPROVED BY THE COMICS CODE AUTHORITY
SUNRISE!

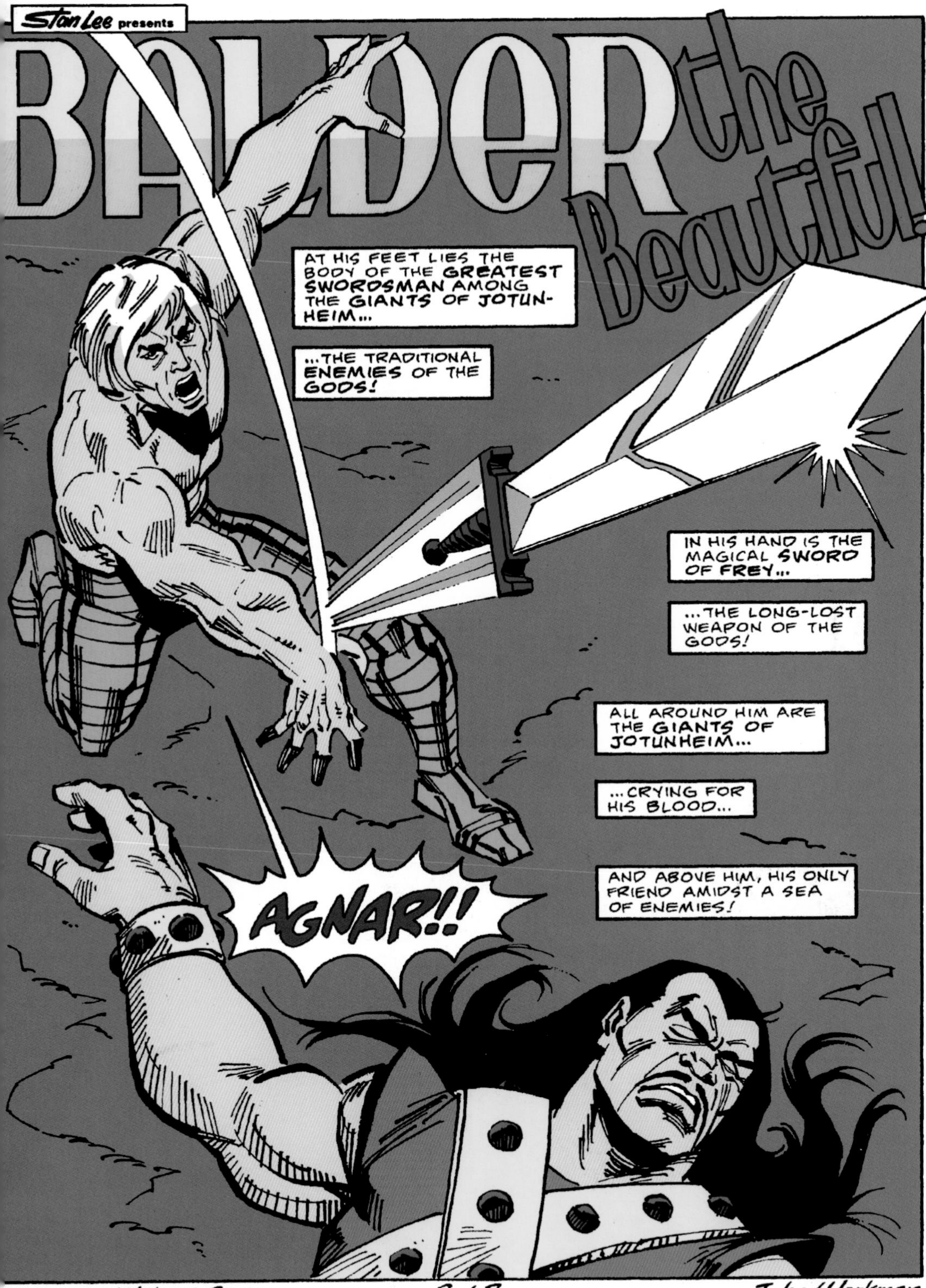
Stan Lee presents
BALDER the Beautiful!
AT HIS FEET LIES THE BODY OF THE GREATEST SWORDSMAN AMONG THE GIANTS OF JOTUNHEIM...
...THE TRADITIONAL ENEMIES OF THE GODS!
IN HIS HAND IS THE MAGICAL SWORD OF FREY...
...THE LONG-LOST WEAPON OF THE GODS!
ALL AROUND HIM ARE THE GIANTS OF JOTUNHEIM...
...CRYING FOR HIS BLOOD...
AND ABOVE HIM, HIS ONLY FRIEND AMIDST A SEA OF ENEMIES!
AGNAR!!

WRITTEN BY Walter Simonson DRAWN BY Sal Buscema LETTERED BY John Workman
COLORED BY Paul Becton EDITED BY Ralph Macchio EDITED IN CHIEF BY Jim Shooter

BALDER HATH SURRENDERED HIS BLADE WITHOUT A **WORD!**

HE IS DEFENSE-LESS! WHAT MEANS THIS RIDDLE?

**HOLD, SCUM!**

THROW DOWN THAT SWORD AND **DESCEND** FROM THY LOFTY PERCH...

...ELSE I SHALL **SLAY** THE **NORN QUEEN** WHOSE LIFE I HOLD IN MY VERY HANDS!

SPOKEN LIKE A TRUE FROST GIANT, UTGARD-LOKI!

EVER COURAGEOUS IN THE FACE OF OVER-WHELMING ODDS!

BUT THE LIFE OF KARNILLA MEANS **NOTHING** TO AGNAR OF VANAHEIM!

FAREWELL, BALDER! MY THANKS FOR THE GIFT!

KILL HIM, BROTHERS!

**SKRAAASHH!**

HE HAS ESCAPED!

SLAY THE QUEEN!

DEATH TO KARNILLA!

HOLD, MY SUBJECTS! LET NOT YOUR WRATH OVERWHELM YOUR REASON!

ALL THE WAYS OF JOTUNHEIM ARE OURS AND HOW SHALL SUCH A LITTLE GOD ESCAPE THEM, MAGIC BLADE OR NO?

AS FOR THE LADY, SHE IS STILL OUR HOSTAGE AGAINST BALDER!

BIND HIM WELL AND TAKE HIM TO THE DEEPEST DUNGEONS!

AND REMEMBER, BALDER, I WILL HOLD KARNILLA'S LIFE AGAINST THY GOOD BE- HAVIOR!

BLOK! COME HITHER.

AGNAR HAS SHOWN US THE MEASURE OF THESE GODS, BLOK.

I DOUBT THAT EVEN FOR A HOSTAGE LIKE BALDER WILL THEY SUR- RENDER THEIR KINGDOM...

...AND I DEEM BALDER TOO DANGEROUS A PRISONER TO HOLD IN ANY CASE.

NOW WHILE HE STILL THINKS WE WISH TO KEEP HIM ALIVE IS THE TIME TO STRIKE.

TAKE TWO OTHERS AND SLAY THE SHINING ONE! QUICKLY!

YOU GIANTS, TAKE YOUR WEAPONS AND SEEK OUT THIS AGNAR.

BUT CAREFULLY! DO NOT SEEK TO KILL HIM FOR THE BLADE OF FREY WILL GUARD HIM AGAINST ANY ATTACK.

MERELY FIND HIM AND KEEP HIM AT BAY WITH PIKES AND SPEARS!

THE COLD WILL DO THE REST!

FOR FROM MY TOWER I WILL WORK MY MAGIC UPON THE REALM.

NO ROAD WILL LEAD HIM ANY-WHERE BUT **BACK** TO THIS CASTLE!

NO TREE WILL GIVE HIM SHELTER.

AND **BITTER** SHALL IT BE THIS NIGHT IN JOTUNHEIM!

METHINKS THE WIND GROWS COLDER BY THE SECOND!

ODIN GRANT THAT I HAVE READ BALDER'S RIDDLE RIGHTLY.

FOR WHEN HE THREW THE BLADE OF FREY TO ME, HE ALSO PASSED THE TORCH.

SURELY, UTGARD-LOKI WOULD HAVE SLAIN KARNILLA, HAD BALDER TRIED TO ESCAPE.

AND BALDER COULD NOT ABANDON THE WOMAN HE LOVES TO CERTAIN DEATH.

BUT CAN I NOW ABANDON HIM?

YET ASGARD MUST BE WARNED THAT THE FROST GIANTS ARE PLANNING TO ATTACK THE GOLDEN REALM NOW THAT ODIN IS GONE.*

AND WHATEVER THE COST, BALDER HAS CHOSEN **ME** TO CARRY THE WARNING!

I SHALL NOT FAIL HIM!

*THAT WAS WAY BACK IN THOR 353 IF YOU WEREN'T PAYING ATTENTION! AND SHAME ON YOU!--RM

BUT WHERE IS OUR CAMP? ONLY THERE SHALL I FIND SUPPLIES THAT WILL ENABLE ME TO REACH ASGARD AND I CAN BARELY SEE MY HAND BE-FORE MY FACE.

HERE RUNS SOME **TRACK** THROUGH THESE ICY WASTES!

IT SEEMS TO BE LEADING ME IN THE DIRECTION I WISH TO GO.

UP AHEAD! THOSE **SHADOWS!** HAVE I FOUND THE FOREST OF DEAD TREES THAT HIDES OUR CAMP OR...?

WHILE NOT FAR AWAY IN THE HIGHEST TOWER OF UTGARD-LOKI'S FORTRESS...

ABIDE HERE AWHILE, KARNILLA. AND IF YOU ARE PATIENT, YOU WILL SEE SECRETS OF GIANT MAGIC THAT NO BEING OUTSIDE THE SELECT OF THIS REALM HAVE EVER WITNESSED.

NATURALLY, YOU'LL NOT BE SHARING THIS KNOWLEDGE WITH ANYONE!

THE STRIPLING AGNAR THINKS TO FLEE JOTUNHEIM AND WARN ASGARD!

YET MANY LEAGUES LIE BETWEEN HIM AND THE BORDERS OF THE KINGDOM HE SEEKS TO ESCAPE.

AND THE GIANTS AND THEIR WORLD ARE AS ONE BEING, BOUND TOGETHER BY BONDS OF ICE AND HATRED THAT YOU CANNOT IMAGINE!

ALREADY, I HAVE CALLED UPON THE NIGHT AND BID HER GROW COLDER!

AND NOW, WITH THESE MAGIKS, I COMMAND IT!

SOON, IT SHALL BE SO ICY THAT A WARM-BLOODED CREATURE WILL PERISH WHILE THE FROST GIANTS ONLY GROW STRONGER!

I DARE SAY THAT EVEN BALDER IN HIS CELL BELOW WILL FEEL THE STING OF THE COLD, FOR ALL HIS VAUNTED WARMTH!

SARRACCKK!

AND AGNAR'S FROZEN BODY SHALL BE FOUND BESIDE THE SWORD OF FREY!

MEANWHILE...

149

INCREDIBLE! THE TRAIL HAS LED ME BACK TO UTGARD-LOKI'S DOOR-STEP AGAIN!

THE PATHS I SEE ARE OBVIOUSLY ILLUSIONS!

IF I CANNOT FIND OUR CAMP SOON, ALL THE POWER OF THE MAGIC SWORD WILL DO ME NO GOOD!

WHAT'S *THAT* IN THE SKY? WHITE-FACE, FATHER OF EAGLES, WHO GUIDED MY FOOTSTEPS TO SAFETY ONCE BEFORE*!

OR ARE YOU AN ILLUSION, TOO?

*AN ISSUE OR TWO AGO--RM

NO! I DO NOT BELIEVE IT! NO GIANT MAGIC WOULD SEEM SO FAIR!

YOU BRAVE THE BITTER COLD TO FLY BEFORE ME LIKE A BEACON, LIGHTING THE WAY TO SAFETY!

AND THOUGH YOU BID ME CROSS A THOUSAND CHASMS LIKE THIS ONE, I WILL FOLLOW WITHOUT HESITATION!

FOR YOUR EYES SEE MORE CLEARLY THAN MINE, FATHER EAGLE.

AND SO SAYING, AGNAR OF VANAHEIM STEPS BRAVELY INTO SPACE AND DISAPPEARS INTO THE SWIRLING CLOUDS OF SNOW.

WHILE SOMEWHERE BEHIND HIM IN THE DEPTHS OF UTGARD-LOKI'S CASTLE...

HERE'S YER ROOM, SHRIMP!

HAR! HAR! HAR!

MAYBE WE'LL SEND A BLANKET IF WE DON'T FORGET!

HAR! HAR! HAR!

KUNNNKK

150

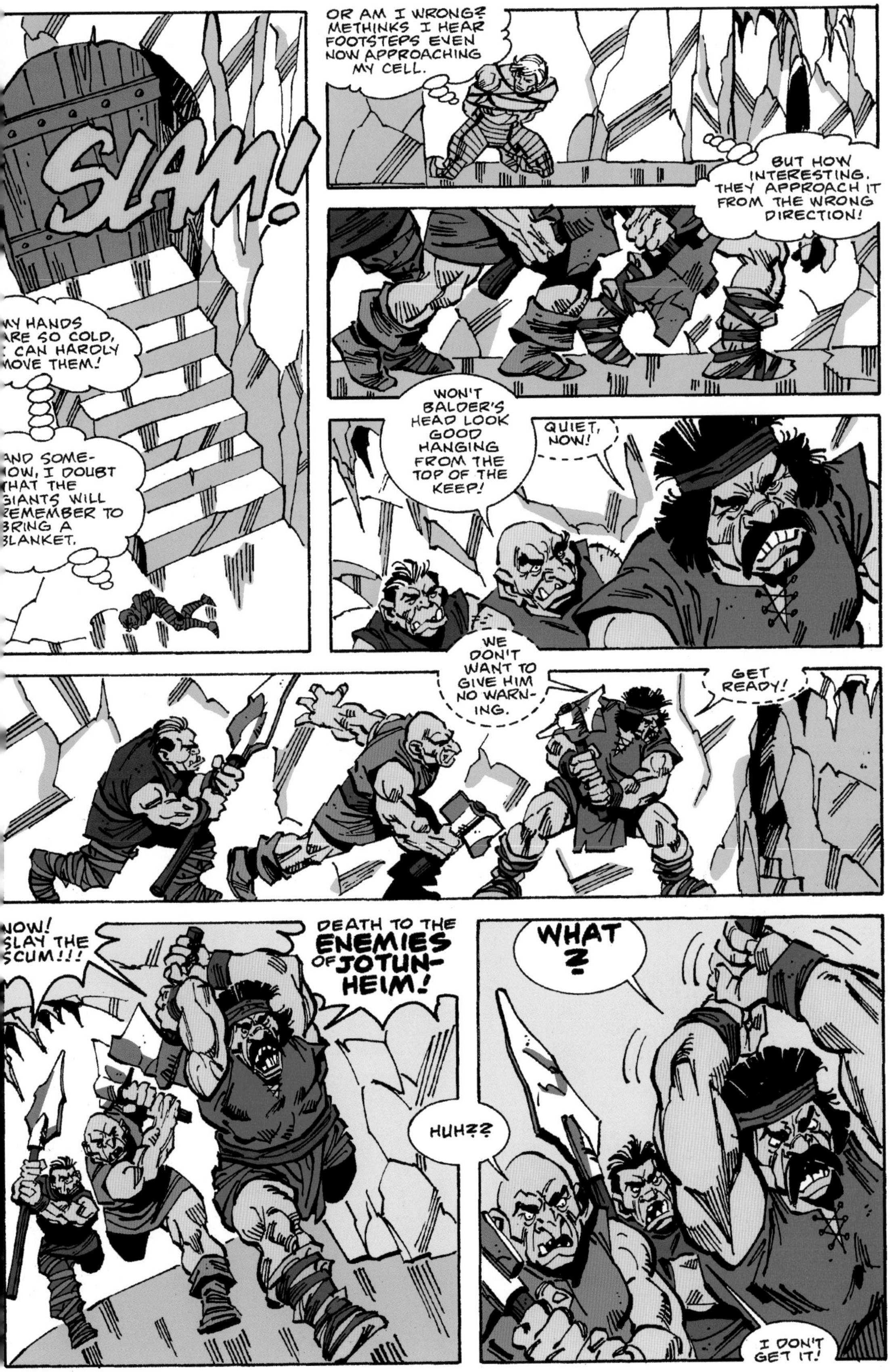
SLAM!
OR AM I WRONG? METHINKS I HEAR FOOTSTEPS EVEN NOW APPROACHING MY CELL.
BUT HOW INTERESTING. THEY APPROACH IT FROM THE WRONG DIRECTION!
MY HANDS ARE SO COLD, I CAN HARDLY MOVE THEM!
AND SOMEHOW, I DOUBT THAT THE GIANTS WILL REMEMBER TO BRING A BLANKET.
WON'T BALDER'S HEAD LOOK GOOD HANGING FROM THE TOP OF THE KEEP!
QUIET, NOW!
WE DON'T WANT TO GIVE HIM NO WARNING.
GET READY!
NOW! SLAY THE SCUM!!!
DEATH TO THE ENEMIES OF JOTUNHEIM!
WHAT?
HUH??
I DON'T GET IT!

WHERE'S HE GONE? WHAT HAPPENED TO THE LITTLE GOD?

FOOL! CAN'T YOU FEEL THE HEAT?

HE'S MELTED HIS CHAINS AND BURNED HIS WAY THROUGH THE WALL!!

BALDER HAS ESCAPED!

OH, THE CHIEF ISN'T GOING TO LIKE THIS!

SO YOU SEE, KARNILLA, THE MEREST ADDITION OF SHREDDED RAM'S BLADDER COMPLETES THE UNIVERSAL SOLVENT!

I SHOULD SAY IN ANOTHER CENTURY OR TWO--

PLEASE, MY LORD, SPARE YOUR SERVANT!

I BRING TERRIBLE NEWS!

HOW NOW?

SHATTERRK!

THEN THE TIME HAS COME FOR US TO BE RID OF THIS TINY PEST ONCE AND FOR ALL!

'TIS THE PRISONER, UTGARD-LOKI! BALDER HATH ESCAPED BOTH HIS CELL AND THY ASSASSINS!

KERASSH!

152

WELL THROWN, GOOD UTGARD! BUT THY REFLEXES ARE NOT A MATCH FOR THY INTENTIONS!

AND YOU'LL NOT HAVE A SECOND CHANCE!

STAND BACK, YOU FOOLS!

SHAKKERT!

SEKASSH!

SHATTER!

LOOK OUT! THE CHEMICALS HAVE SPARKED A BLAZING FIRE!

ARRGH! MY FACE!

WHERE IS THE ASGARDIAN SCUM?

I'LL HAVE HIM FLAYED ALIVE FOR THIS!

NOW, BEFORE HE THINKS TO USE KARNILLA AGAINST ME IS THE TIME TO ACT!

AND UTGARD-LOKI HAS UNWITTINGLY GIVEN ME THE MEANS TO REACH HER!

SHE RESTS IMPRISONED UPON YON TABLE...

MMMMPH!

KARNILLA!

BOUND AND GAGGED TO PREVENT HER FROM USING ANY MAGIC, I'LL WARRANT!

BUT SHE SEEMS UNHARMED!

TURN AWAY, MY QUEEN...

...AND I SHALL SHATTER YOUR PRISON!

KARRRACK

AND NOW -- WHAT?

THE FLAMES HAVE BEEN EXTINGUISHED, GODLING, AND YOUR TIME HAS RUN OUT!

UTGARD-LOKI!

YOU AND KARNILLA SHALL SHARE THE FATE OF HER ENTIRE KINGDOM!

PERHAPS YOU SHOULD EMBRACE...

...FOR THE DEADLY DUST OF UTGARD-LOKI SHALL TURN YOU TO STONE... FOREVER!

...AND ENJOY EACH OTHER'S CARESSES ETERNALLY...

WE HAVE BUT ONE CHANCE!

IF I CAN IGNITE THE POWDER BEFORE WE IN-HALE IT, WE MAY YET AVOID THIS TERRIBLE DOOM!

SHARROAMM!

MY DUST! BALDER'S BURNING RAYS ARE CAUSING IT TO EXPLODE!

AND THE HEAT WITHIN THE TOWER BIDS FAIR TO BECOME UNBEARABLE!

THE TRICK HAS WORKED! KARNILLA AND I ARE STILL FLESH AND BLOOD!

BUT I MUST RADIATE ALL THE ENERGY I CAN, LEST ANY OF THE DUST REMAIN!

EVERY ATOM OF THAT DEADLY PLAGUE MUST BE CONSUMED!

BALDER, FORBEAR! THY HEAT IS MORE THAN WE CAN STAND!

MERCY!

SURELY MY EYES DECEIVE THEMSELVES! FOR EVEN AS I GLOW HOTTER AND HOTTER, THE ROOM ABOUT ME SEEMS TO SHRINK!

NAY, I SEE IT CLEARLY NOW!

I HAVE BROUGHT LIGHT AND HEAT TO A LAND WHERE THE SUN IN ALL ITS GLORY NEVER SHINES!

THE ROOM, THIS VERY CASTLE ITSELF, IS MELTING!

GAGGG-GKAGK!

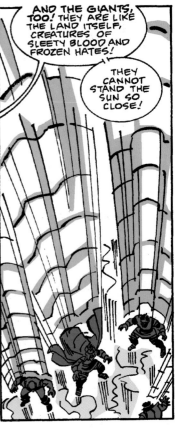

AND THE GIANTS, TOO! THEY ARE LIKE THE LAND ITSELF, CREATURES OF SLEETY BLOOD AND FROZEN HATES!

THEY CANNOT STAND THE SUN SO CLOSE!

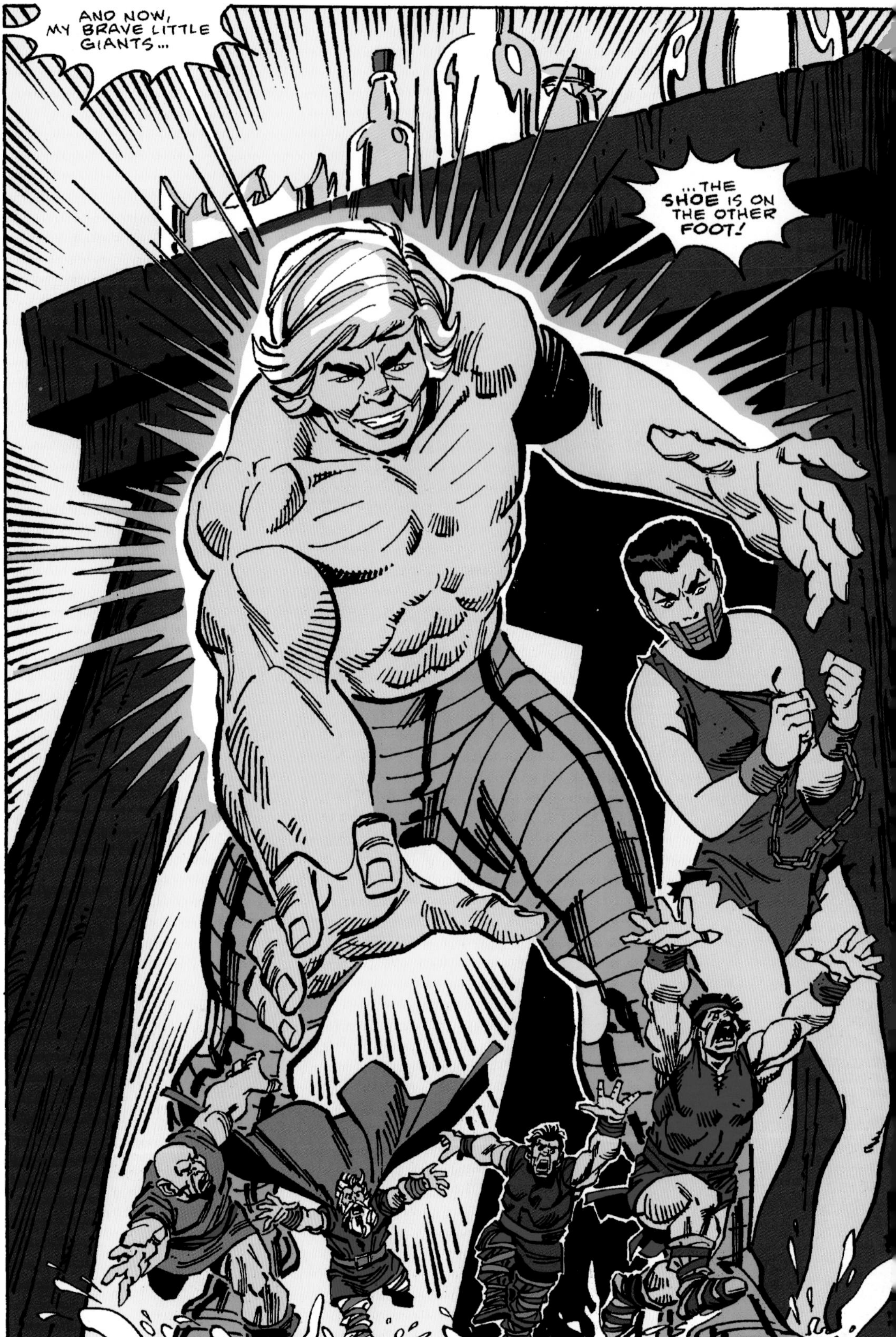
AND NOW, MY BRAVE LITTLE GIANTS...
...THE SHOE IS ON THE OTHER FOOT!

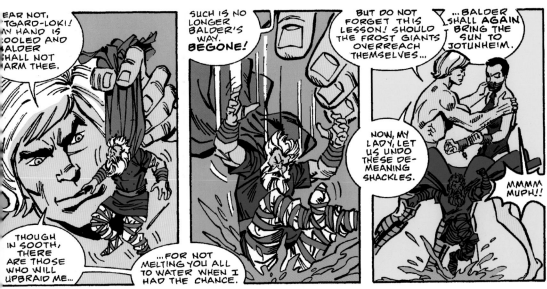

FEAR NOT, 'TGARD-LOKI! MY HAND IS COOLED AND BALDER SHALL NOT HARM THEE.

SUCH IS NO LONGER BALDER'S WAY. BEGONE!

BUT DO NOT FORGET THIS LESSON! SHOULD THE FROST GIANTS OVERREACH THEMSELVES...

...BALDER SHALL AGAIN BRING THE SUN TO JOTUNHEIM.

NOW, MY LADY, LET US UNDO THESE DE-MEANING SHACKLES.

MMMM MUPH!!

THOUGH, IN SOOTH, THERE ARE THOSE WHO WILL UPBRAID ME...

...FOR NOT MELTING YOU ALL TO WATER WHEN I HAD THE CHANCE.

FREE AT LAST! RUN, 'TGARD-LOKI! RUN, YOU CUR, BUT NO MATTER HOW FAR YOU GO...

...NOWHERE SHALL BE FAR ENOUGH THAT I SHALL NOT FIND YOU AND MAKE YOU PAY FOR THE IN-DIGNITIES I HAVE SUFFERED!

KARNILLA! PLEASE, MY LOVE, LET THEM GO.

IS THIS WHAT BALDER WISHES? THAT THE ENEMIES WHO STOLE KARNILLA AND LAID WASTE HER KINGDOM SHOULD GO FREE?

THE GIANTS' CASTLE HAS BEEN DESTROYED. THEY, THEMSELVES, HAVE BEEN SO REDUCED IN SIZE THAT THEY HAVE BEEN RENDERED HARMLESS.

SHOULD WE STILL SEEK THEIR LIVES? COME.

AND SHORTLY...

THESE BORROWED FURS SHALL WARM US TILL WE REACH NORNREALM,

THOUGHTS OF UTGARD-LOKI RUNNING FREE SHALL KEEP ME BURN-ING!

IS OUR ONLY CHOICE, THEN, TO BECOME LIKE THE FROST GIANTS...

...LIVING IN HATE AND DESTROYING EVERYTHING WE CANNOT LOVE?

IF I THOUGHT, OH QUEEN, THAT YOU WERE NO MORE THAN A FROST GIANT IN A BEAUTIFUL DISGUISE, I SHOULD NOT LOVE YOU.

BALDER, WHAT'S THAT?

'TIS RATTUSK! THE VERY DEMON I... THAT IS... THE DEMON WHOM YOU DID BID ME SPARE WHEN YOU FIRST LEFT MY KINGDOM *.

YOUR FAITH IN HIM WAS REWARDED AS YOU DESERVED, LADY.

*BALDER No. 1

ALONE OF ALL HIS FELLOWS, HE AVOIDED THE DEADLY DUST OF STONE AND FOLLOWED THE GIANTS WHO KIDNAPPED YOU BACK TO THEIR LAIR.

AND YOUR ARMOR?

HE WORE IT TO LAY A FALSE TRAIL FOR THE GIANTS, ENABLING ME TO ENTER THE GREAT FORTRESS.

THE GIANTS SLEW HIM. HE DIED AS HE LIVED.

I AM TOO TIRED TO TAKE US HOME WITH MAGIC, BALDER, BUT YOUR ARMOR I CAN REPAIR.

PLEASE, FOR MY SAKE, DO NOT LEAVE POOR RATTUSK FOR THE SAVAGE BEASTS.

AND SHORTLY...

'TIS DONE, LADY, NOW LET US DEPART THIS BITTER LAND.

SOME TIME LATER, MANY LEAGUES AWAY IN THE DESERTED AND FORLORN KINGDOM OF NORNREALM...

WHITEFACE HAS DONE IT! I HAVE REACHED KARNILLA'S CASTLE...

...BUT MY FOOD IS GONE, MY WATER BAG NEARLY EMPTY...

ODIN GRANT SOME SUPPLIES YET REMAIN HERE, THAT I MIGHT FINISH THE JOURNEY TO ASGARD AND WARN HER OF HER PERIL!

THIS GUARD-HOUSE SEEMS UNDISTURBED, MAYBE I CAN FIND--

A SHADOW! NORNKEEP IS NOT SO DESERTED AS IT SEEMS!

STAND, VILLAIN!

I RIDE FOR ASGARD AND NOTHING SHALL PREVENT ME FROM REACHING MY APPOINTED GOAL!

SO IT WOULD SEEM, AGNAR OF VANAHEIM, LEAST OF ALL ME.

HOGUN THE GRIM!!

WHEN LAST WE MET, WARRIOR, YOU WERE A CALLOW YOUTH.

NOW I PERCEIVE A MARKED CHANGE IN THINE EYES.

AND I RECOGNIZE THE FABLED BLADE YOU BEAR.

BALDER GAVE IT INTO MY CARE!

INDEED. HERE, EAT, I WILL SEE TO THY HORSE.

AND SHORTLY...

'TIS SAID THE BLADE OF FREY WILL NOT TOLERATE THE UNJUST, BUT HAS EVER PROVEN TO BE THEIR BANE.

WELL... I HAVEN'T ACTUALLY HAD TO USE IT YET.

NO MATTER, I THINK IT WILL PERMIT YOU TO WIELD IT, SHOULD THE NEED ARISE.

NOW... TELL ME OF BALDER.

IN A FEW SHORT WORDS, AGNAR TELLS HOGUN OF BALDER'S JOURNEY INTO JOTUNHEIM*.

*THE TALE OF THE LAST TWO ISSUES--RM

AND I KNOW NOT WHETHER BALDER IS NOW ALIVE OR DEAD.

BUT HE ENTRUSTED ME TO CARRY THE WORD TO ASGARD AND I WILL NOT FAIL HIM.

WHY DID YOU COME TO SEARCH FOR HIM IN NORN-REALM?

...AND BALDER HATH BEEN DECLARED THE NEW LORD OF THE GOLDEN REALM.

WHAT?! BALDER KING?!

THE GREAT ALTHING HAS MET IN ASGARD...*

THORS 365/366--RM

AYE, I HAD COME TO BRING HIM HOME.

NOW, WE MUST MAKE HASTE TO ASGARD, BUT I SHALL LEAVE MY MESSAGE BEHIND.

FOR BALDER IS A VALIANT AND NOBLE WARRIOR...

...AND IF ANY CAN WIN THROUGH THE GIANTS OF JOTUNHEIM, 'TWILL BE HE!

BY THIS BLADE, HE WILL KNOW THAT HOGUN HATH BEEN HERE.

COME, AGNAR, IF THOU ART REFRESHED.

ASGARD SHALL BE **WARNED!**

MEANWHILE, IN THE FORESTS BEYOND THE REACH OF THE ICY WINDS OF JOTUNHEIM...

YOU ARE QUIET TO-NIGHT, MY LOVE.

DO YOU STILL DREAM OF UTGARD-LOKI AND HIS DE-STRUCTION?

I STILL WONDER WHAT KIND OF **LOVE** FOR ME YOU BEAR THAT HOLDS YOUR HAND FROM STRIKING AT MY ENEMIES.

HAVE YOU NOT CONSIDERED, KARNILLA, THAT SOMETIMES THERE IS MORE CRUELTY IN KIND-NESS?

WHAT DO YOU MEAN?

PERHAPS IT WILL BE ALL THE MORE PAINFUL FOR UTGARD-LOKI AND HIS MINIONS TO LIVE THUS...

...IN BODIES THAT WILL **MATCH** THEIR PETTINESS OF SPIRIT...

...DWELLING UPON THE BITTER MEMORIES OF THIS DEFEAT.

THEY WILL NOT BE MARTYRS TO AN EVIL CAUSE; THEY WILL BE LAUGH-INGSTOCKS.

AND HE AND HIS MINIONS SHALL SERVE AS LIVING EXAMPLES TO FROST GIANTS EVERYWHERE NOT TO SET THEMSELVES AGAINST THE WILL OF THE GODS.

I SOME-TIMES WONDER, BALDER, WHICH OF US IS THE CRUELER.

160

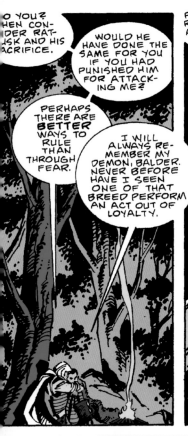

O YOU? HEN CON- DER RAT- JSK AND HIS ACRIFICE.

WOULD HE HAVE DONE THE SAME FOR YOU IF YOU HAD PUNISHED HIM FOR ATTACK- ING ME?

PERHAPS THERE ARE **BETTER** WAYS TO RULE THAN THROUGH FEAR.

I WILL ALWAYS RE- MEMBER MY DEMON, BALDER. NEVER BEFORE HAVE I SEEN ONE OF THAT **BREED** PERFORM AN ACT OUT OF LOYALTY.

PERHAPS YOU ARE RIGHT AND **LOVE** IS A GREATER WEAPON THAN FEAR.

PERHAPS LOVE IS NOT A WEAPON.

IN ANY CASE, I HAVE NO KINGDOM LEFT TO RULE. I AM A QUEEN WITHOUT A COUNTRY.

YET YOU ARE A SORCERESS AS WELL. ONE OF GREAT ABILITY AND RENOWN.

YOUR SUBJECTS STILL EXIST, THE VICTIMS OF A TERRIBLE MAGIC. BUT ARE THEY NOT STILL YOUR SUBJECTS?

ND AS THEY OWE HEIR ALLEGIANCE O THEIR QUEEN, OES NOT THEIR UEEN OWE **HER** LLEGIANCE TO **THEM?**

THE RESPONSI- BILITIES OF THAT HIGH OFFICE ARE NOT LIGHTLY BRUSHED ASIDE.

PERHAPS IT IS WITHIN YOUR POWER TO RE- STORE THEM TO LIFE.

DO NOT KNOW, BALDER, WATCHED UTGARD-LOKI AREFULLY AND KNOW MUCH ORE NOW THAN FORMERLY OF GIANT MAGIC...

...AND THIS MUCH I HAVE LEARNED. THE ENCHANTMENTS OF THE GIANTS ARE VERY **DIFFERENT** FROM MY OWN.

BUT YOU ARE RIGHT. I **SHALL** ATTEMPT IT. AND PERHAPS, SOMEDAY, I SHALL SUCCEED.

AND YOU?

NEVER FEAR, MY QUEEN, BALDER SHALL STAY BY YOUR SIDE.

I HAVE NOT JOURNEYED ALL THE WAY INTO JOTUNHEIM TO CAST ASIDE THE PRIZE AND RETURN TO MY SILENT HALL IN ASGARD.

SOMETIME LATER...
THE GATES OF NORNREALM AT LAST!

IT SEEMS AN AGE SINCE I WAS CARRIED THROUGH THEM BY THE GIANTS OF UTGARD-LOKI.

I HARDLY FEEL LIKE THE SAME WOMAN.

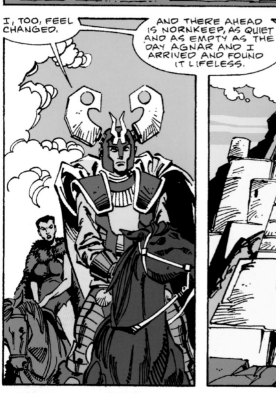

I, TOO, FEEL CHANGED.

AND THERE AHEAD IS NORNKEEP, AS QUIET AND AS EMPTY AS THE DAY AGNAR AND I ARRIVED AND FOUND IT LIFELESS.

YET YOUR PEOPLE ARE ALL HERE, AWAITING YOUR RETURN.

THEIR WAITING WILL BE OVER SOMEDAY. I SWEAR IT.

I DO NOT DOUBT IT, KARNILLA.

HO, AGNAR! ARE YOU WITHIN?

NO ANSWER. PERHAPS HE DID NOT ESCAPE THE SNARES OF UTGARD-LOKI.

YET WE SAW NO SIGN OF HIM ON OUR JOURNEY HOME.

WHAT'S THIS I SEE? A KNIFE PINNING SOMETHING TO THE DOOR OF A SILENT GUARDHOUSE?

MY LORD, IF YOU WOULD SEE TO THE HORSES, I WILL PREPARE US A SMALL REPAST TO REFRESH OUR SPIRITS.

WE ARE BOTH TIRED, I THINK.

IS ADDRESSED TO BALDER!

COME, MY BEAUTIES. THERE'S A DRINK AND FRESH HAY FOR YOU IN THE STABLES, IF I'M NOT MISTAKEN.

WELL, PERHAPS NOT SO FRESH, BUT I EXPECT YOU'LL HAVE NO COMPLAINTS.

UNBELIEVABLE! BALDER HATH BEEN CHOSEN **RULER** OF ASGARD! AND THIS NOTE BIDS HIM RETURN TO THE GOLDEN REALM **AT ONCE!**

NO! I'LL NOT STAND FOR IT!

AFTER ALL THAT HAS HAPPENED, SURELY HE AND I DESERVE AN HOUR OF PEACE!

THOR, THOU BLUSTERER! I SHALL NEVER **FORGIVE** THEE FOR NOT TAKING THY RIGHTFUL THRONE!

KARNILLA, THE HORSES ARE STABLED. KARNILLA?

A MESSAGE FOR YOU, BALDER.

FOR ME? I RECOGNIZE THIS DAGGER, IT BELONGS TO HOGUN.

"AND AS THEY OWE THEIR ALLEGIANCE TO THEIR QUEEN, DOES NOT THEIR QUEEN OWE **HER** ALLEGIANCE TO THEM?"

THAT IS TRUE OF **KINGS** AS WELL, IS IT NOT, BALDER?

WHAT CAN YOU SAY, MY LOVE? YOU ARE AS **TRAPPED** BY YOUR WORDS AS I.

KARNILLA.

DO NOT **SHATTER** MY FAITH. DO NOT ASK ME TO RETURN WITH YOU TO ASGARD. IS MY PLACE NOT HERE?

ONCE, A LIFETIME AGO, I WITHHELD SOMETHING THAT WOULD HAVE BEEN A HELP TO YOU.

AND SO THE GIANTS FOUND THE SWORD OF FREY IN MY ARMORY.

IT IS MY GIFT TO YOU, NOW. HAD I BEEN LESS SELFISH EARLIER, OUR FATES MIGHT HAVE BEEN DIFFERENT.

ODIN HIMSELF MIGHT STILL RULE ASGARD, AND I WOULD NOT BE LOSING YOU.

I AM SURE AGNAR KEEPS IT IN TRUST FOR YOU EVEN NOW.

SOMEDAY, IT MAY BRING YOU BACK SAFELY TO ME.

TAKE MY RING, TOO, THAT BALDER MIGHT REMEMBER HIS KARNILLA AND KNOW THAT WHEREVER HE IS, HER THOUGHTS ARE WITH HIM.

NOW **GO**, MY LOVE, BEFORE I FORGET THAT I AM A QUEEN AND NOT A WOMAN.

164

…AVE THE HOOFBEATS OF BALDER'S STEED, THERE IS NO SOUND AT ALL IN NORNREALM…

…AS **BALDER THE BRAVE** RIDES FORTH INTO THE DAY TO ASSUME THE MANTLE OF LIEGE LORD OF THE GOLDEN REALM OF ASGARD.

AND AT NIGHT, THE ONLY SOUND IS THAT OF THE RAIN SOFTLY FALLING WITHIN KARNILLA'S CHAMBERS.

*Fin*

AND A LAST TIP OF THE HORNED HELMET FROM BALDER AND THE BOYS. IT'S BEEN FUN, FOLKS. --RALPH, WALT AND SAL.

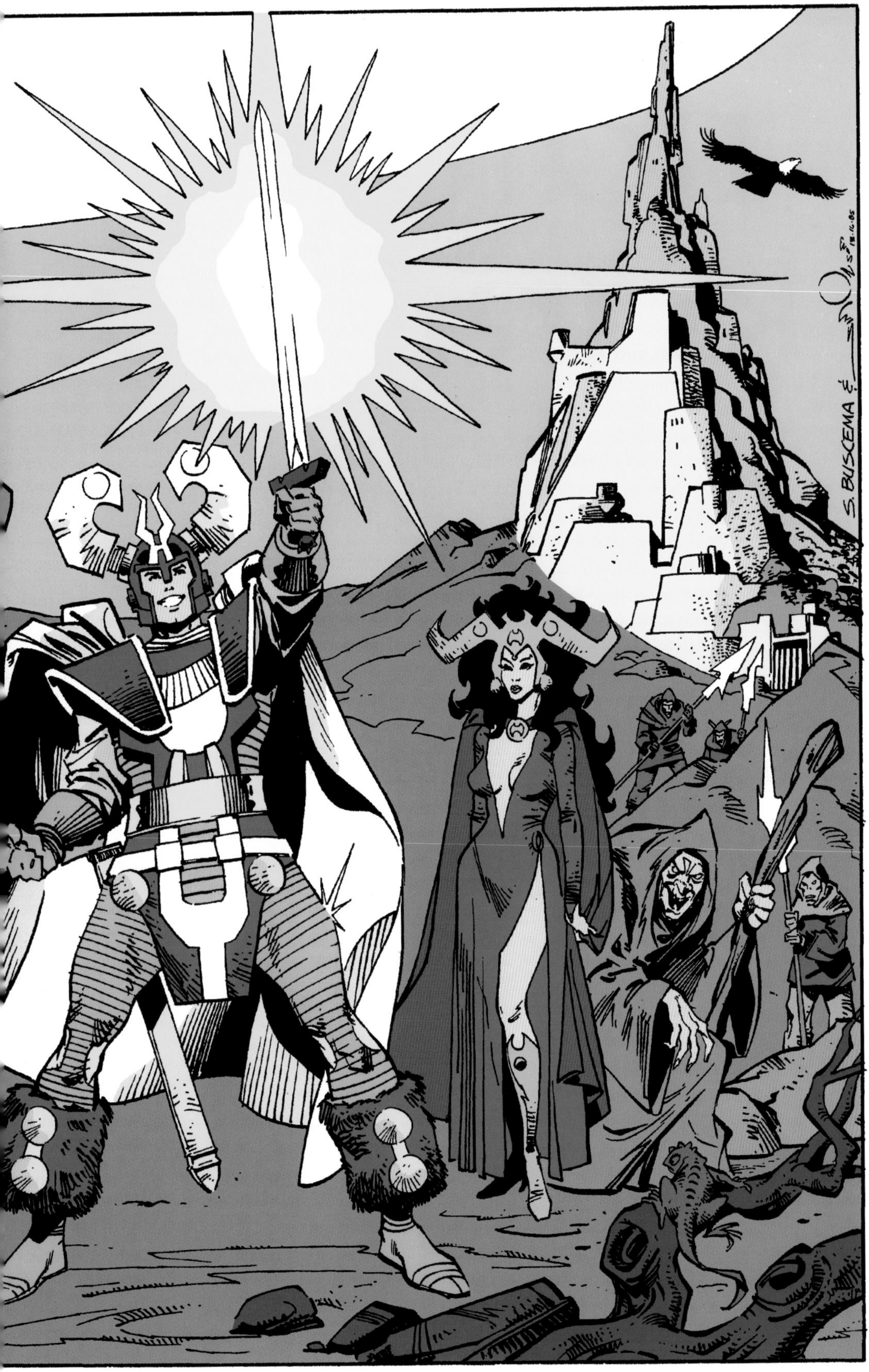
S. BUSCEMA

# AN EPIC OF LOVE AND WAR . . .

# Balder And Karnilla ™

by **Dwight Jon Zimmerman**

The history of literature is rich with the records of the great struggles endured by men and women united by love, but cruelly separated by fate, circumstance and sometimes their immutable beliefs: **Orpheus**, bravely singing before the Lord of the Dead himself to win the return of his wife, **Eurydice**, to the land of the living; the star-crossed romance between **Tristan**, **King Arthur's** strongest knight, and the fair **Isolde**; and now that of Asgard's noblest warrior, **Balder**, with the Norn realm's imperious queen, **Karnilla**, in the epic four-issue Limited Series, **BALDER AND KARNILLA**.

Written by **Walt Simonson** and penciled and inked by **Sal Buscema**, this bi-monthly Limited Series not only probes and reveals the tempestuous, paradoxical and seemingly contradictory romance that has tortured the lives of both **Balder** and **Karnilla**, it also heralds a new war that is about to sweep an Asgard struggling to rebuild itself after its brush with annihilation at the hand of **Surtur**.

Series editor, **Ralph Macchio**, stated that the events chronicled in the Limited Series will be closely tied with **THOR** beginning with the story in **THOR** #260. And, **Ralph** said, "BALDER AND KARNILLA will have a number of themes. Politics — the relationship of political power with some of the sleazy things going on in Asgard, and the strength of one man's — or god's — uncorruptable will and how it can bend almost anything if he so chooses. And it is also about the redemption of character."

**Ralph** added, "It's really going to be what a Limited Series should be. It will develop the characters to their fullest potential. **Walt** is going to be using the Limited Series to focus on **Balder**, on his character, on his relationship with **Karnilla** and on what is going to happen in Asgard. He's really going to say something in this Limited Series about politics and interpersonal relation-

ships — with a lot of fighting in between."

Because **BALDER AND KARNILLA** will be so closely intertwined with what will be happening in **THOR**, **Walt** offered this background to show what led up to the Limited Series and how he arranged for it to fit in to the continuity of **THOR**. "What I've tried to do in **THOR** is present the stories in a way that suggests the old Icelandic sagas –– which is where a lot of information

WOULD HE EVEN NEED SUCH A WEAPON?

we have about **Thor** and Asgard comes from. To do this, what I've tried to do is set up themes for a cycle of stories. The individual tales are individual stories, but they all have a theme that links them with the other tales. The first cycle of stories was about the war with **Surtur**. At the conclusion of that cycle I tried to set up a new set of problems that would begin the second cycle. That set of problems revolves around the fact that **Odin** is gone. Who rules next in Asgard? That question is what the **THOR** series is now dealing with. This cycle will be resolved around #365; don't shoot me if I miss that by an issue or so. We will then go into the third cycle of stories, called 'The Frost Giant/Asgard War.' **The Frost Giants** are the traditional enemies of the Norse gods, and **Thor**, in particular. In the Marvel version of Norse mythology, when **the Frost Giants** learn that **Odin** is gone, they will figure that now is the perfect time for them to attack and destroy Asgard. This all leads me into the **BALDER AND KARNILLA Limited Series** because the opening salvo of the war will occur in the first issue of the Limited Series."

During the time of the succession to the throne of Asgard, **Balder** has remained in **Karnilla's** realm. And it is in that realm we find him at the opening of the first issue of the Limited Series, talking about the fabled Magic Sword of **Frey** — a sword so powerful that it can cut anything and literally fight by itself! **Frey** lost the sword in his own quest for love. And nobody knows where it went, though many were the attempts to find the weapon. We discover, in that first issue as well, the reason for the searchers' failures — **Karnilla** was the one who stole the sword and it is now resting in the deepest chambers of her armory.

The sword plays an increasingly important role in the Limited Series which sees **Balder** not only become embroiled in the war against **the Frost**

*ARTICLE FROM MARVEL AGE #30 (SEPTEMBER 1985)*

IS AN EXCELLENT BATION, KARNILLA.

SURELY THIS MUST BE SOME RARE WINE PROCURED FROM BEYOND THE SHORES OF RINGSFJORD.

WITH THE PASSING OF DAYS, BRAVE BALDER, YOU MAY YET HAVE A CHANCE TO SAMPLE THE MYRIAD DELIGHTS OF MY ENTIRE CELLAR.

**Giants**, but also involuntarily return to Hel! According to **Walt**, "The reason for this is that some issues back, in **THOR**, I had an episode about some mortals eating some magic cookies. The mortals who ate those cookies had their souls transported to Hel, even though their bodies remained on Earth. At the end of that story, **Thor** vowed to go to Hel and try to save those souls when he had the time to, because they had been taken unjustly. Now that time has come. And **Thor** has not forgotten his promise. The trick about going into Hel is that going down there is not so difficult. A number of people and beings know the way down. But nobody really knows the way back — only **Balder** has entered Hel and lived to return and tell the tale. So **Thor** calls upon **Balder** to give him a hand, to kind of act as a guide, really, to get everyone out again when the time comes."

As you can imagine, this will not be an easy decision for **Balder**. **Balder's** experience in Hel was worse than what anyone believed possible. "But he's going to do it, because he's a noble guy," **Walt** said.

**Balder's** decision to help **Thor** causes an immediate and spiteful reaction from **Karnilla**. She does *not* want **Balder** to go. She cannot countenance losing him again. But **Balder** remains adamant. And, royally miffed because he will not obey her, she witholds from an unsuspecting **Balder** something that she can do to aid him. "She will have cause to regret that," **Walt** said.

The quest into Hel continues on into **THOR**. With the second issue of the Limited Series, **Balder** returns to the Norn realm to discover that it has been ravaged and **Karnilla** kidnapped by **the Frost Giants**. From then on, **Balder**, in the Limited Series, pursues **Karnilla's** captors and does everything he can to try and deflect this, the first blow in **the Frost Giant's** war against Asgard.

But why, since she represents all that he despises, does **Balder** embark on this quest to rescue **Karnilla**? "**Agnar**, the messenger sent by **Thor**, asked **Balder** the same question, 'What do you see in **Karnilla**?'" **Walt** said. "And **Balder** will clearly express his feelings for **Karnilla** in the first

issue." As **Walt** interprets, **Balder** sees the good in **Karnilla**. "She's certainly self-interested," **Walt** said. "But a lot of what she does, she does out of a love for **Balder**. This is maybe her one saving grace." And, as for their relationship in general, **Walt** said, "It's not a precise relationship, which is one of the things I find fascinating about it. We don't quite know what to expect. That's really going to be the dynamic element that I'll be exploring."

**Ralph Macchio** observed, "I think what **Karnilla** sees in the relationship is something about the purity of **Balder**. Something that anyone who lives with corruption loves or wants is something in their life that is incredibly pure. And **Karnilla** sees in **Balder** the purest, most untouchable thing in Asgard. And she wants it for herself." **Walt** quickly agreed, "Oh, definitely. I think that if **Balder** became corrupt and evil, **Karnilla** would lose interest in him. I guess that is one of the things that keeps him eternally fascinating for her."

On **Karnilla**, herself, **Walt** said, "I'd like **Karnilla** to grow during the course of this Limited Series so that we have

COME, MY LITTLE FRIENDS, AND EAT.

FOR HERE WE SHARE OUR FOOD AND FATE, HUDDLED IN THE DARKNESS.

an opportunity to see more of her. One of the reasons you enjoy doing a Limited Series like this is because you can focus on supporting characters who can't get that much attention in the regular series." And **Walt** would like to see **Karnilla** develop enough so that, by the end of the Limited Series, if she was faced with similar circumstances to what she encountered at the beginning of the Limited Series, she would not make the same decisions.

**Walt** is very excited about this multi-level "juggling act" he is performing — wrapping-up the second cycle of stories in the **THOR** series, concurrently beginning a new crisis for Thor in another set of tales, and uncovering new facets in all the characters. It's a big task, but one that **Walt** has completely worked out. "On these stories you have two levels, your personal stories which deal with relationships and conflicts on a close, intimate, level, and then you have the cosmic-level conflict, particularly in **THOR** where you have gods and demons and large-scale events." And once the succession to the throne of Asgard problem is solved, and the Limited Series concludes, the conflict that has been building up in **BALDER AND KARNILLA** will shift over to **THOR** and the Frost Giant/Asgard War will be resolved there.

As anyone who has been reading **THOR** already knows, **Walt's** depiction of the Thunder God has made him one of the most popular artists in comics. The experience he is having coupling his vision with that of another of Marvel's great visualizers, **Sal Buscema**, has been more rewarding than even he anticipated. This happy collaboration began in **THOR** #355. "I had a delightful time working with **Sal** on **THOR**," **Walt** said. "**Sal** gave me everything I asked for — and more. It was a real pleasure to write from his art. **Sal** is one of the guys whose work I read back before I became a professional. And it has been a real personal joy working and talking with him now."

"I'm really having a ball with it!" **Sal Buscema** said. "I just wish that there were more things like **BALDER AND KARNILLA** to do because it is so much fun. I don't mean to say that the other stories I've done aren't, just that this one is really special." Did **Sal** find himself doing the Limited Series differently? "I don't know if you could say I'm approaching it any differently," **Sal** replied. "**BALDER AND KARNILLA** is different in the sense that it's not the usual super hero thing. We are dealing with mythology here. That in itself makes the story different."

One of the points that **Sal** was quick to point out about his and **Walt's** collaboration is that **Walt** has given him

some of the most visually excitin plots he's ever received. "That is wh I'm enjoying working on **Walt's** plot s much," **Sal** said. "He is an illustrate as well as a writer, and I think that h has a sense for pictures that a write alone, doesn't. And I say this not bein derogatory to writers. Writers pair their pictures with words — their think ing is different. **Walt** is thinking i terms of visuals. What kind of picture is this story going to make? What op portunity to do some very powerf and dramatic story-telling pictures ar there in this? Because an artist has th tendency to think more in those term than a writer, **Walt** has made my jo very easy.

"Another thing that has made thi Limited Series such a joy for me is tha **Walt** really does his homework," **S**a added. "He's researched his subjec very well and knows what he's doing That in itself is the foundation for som very good storytelling. I have a feelin that **Walt** is becoming the authority o Norse mythology."

For his part, **Walt** said, "I think tha **Sal** is now doing the best work of hi career. This is very heartening to guy like me who are younger than **Sal**, t see guys like him who have been i the business for so many years an see that they *are* doing better tha ever."

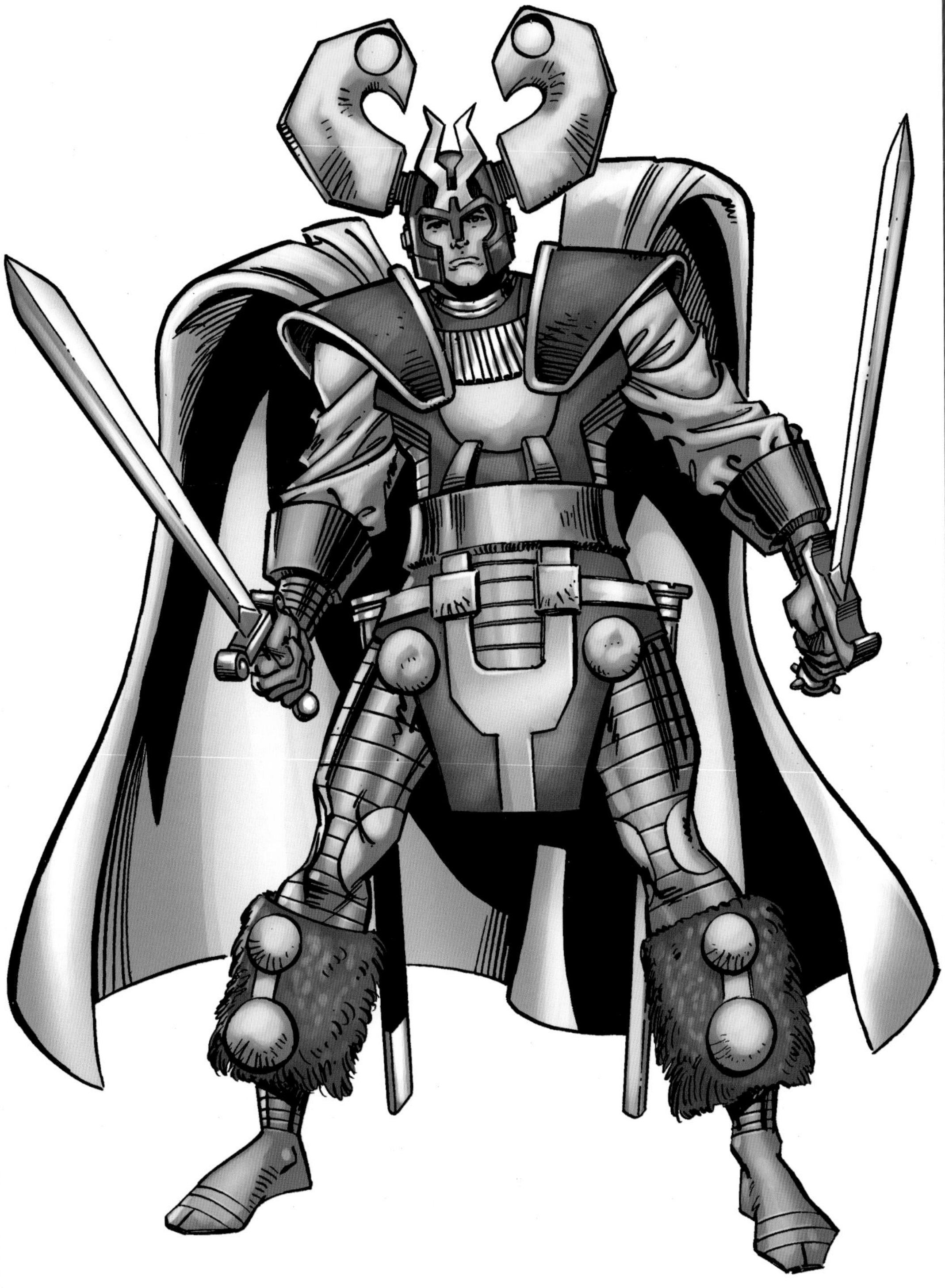

# BALDER

**Real Name:** Balder
**Occupation:** Warrior-god, Asgardian god of light
**Identity:** Publicly known on Earth, although the general public of Earth does not believe him to be the god of Norse mythology.
**Legal status:** Citizen of Asgard
**Other current aliases:** Balder the Brave

**Place of birth:** Asgard
**Marital status:** Single
**Known relatives:** None
**Group affiliation:** Gods of Asgard, frequent personal ally of Thor and the Warriors Three
**Base of operations:** Asgard
**First appearance:** JOURNEY INTO MYSTERY #85

**History:** Due to his many heroic deeds over the ages, Balder has long been regarded as Asgard's noblest god and its greatest warrior next to the thunder god Thor, who has long been Balder's closest friend (see *Asgard*). Balder has been unsuccessfully sought as a lover by the sorceress Karnilla the Norn Queen (see *Karnilla*).

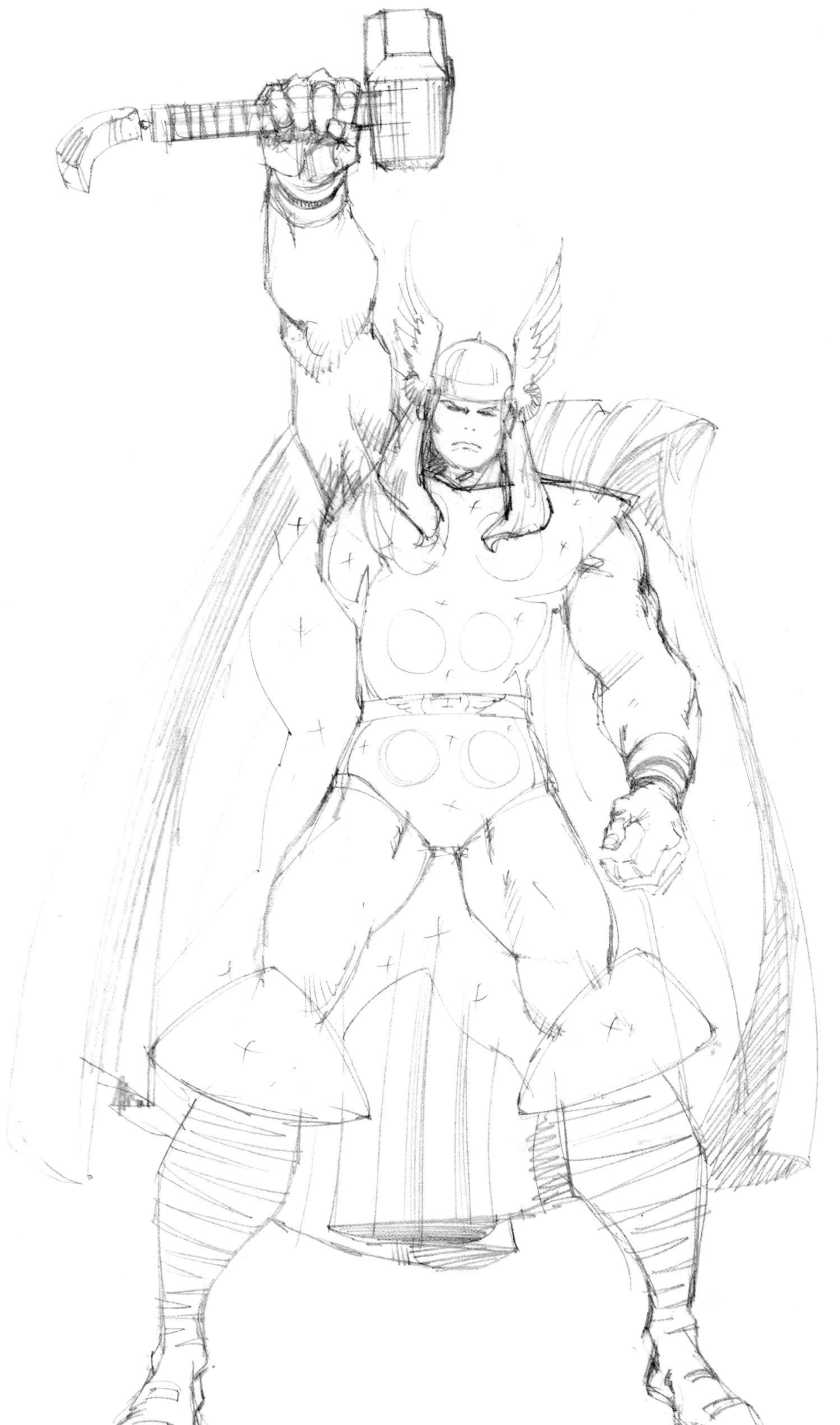

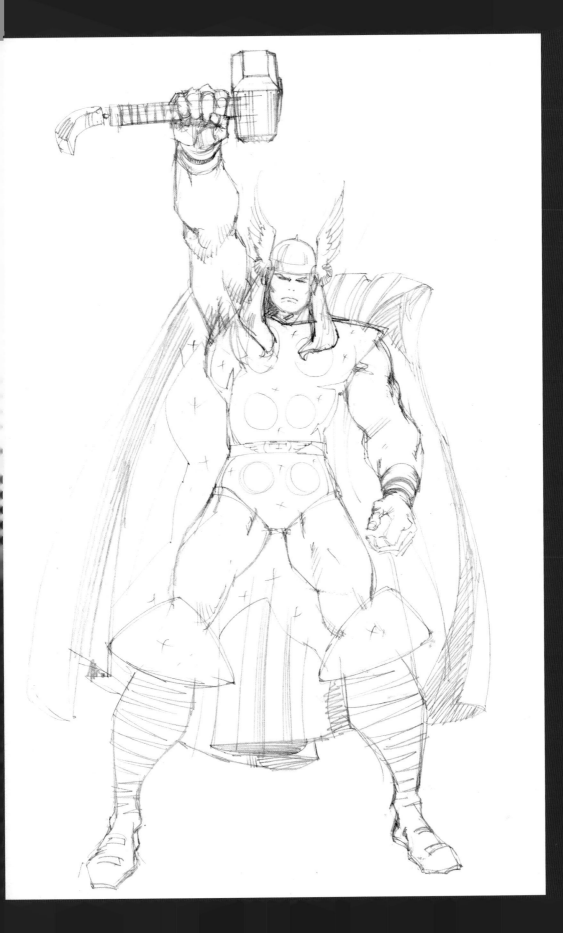

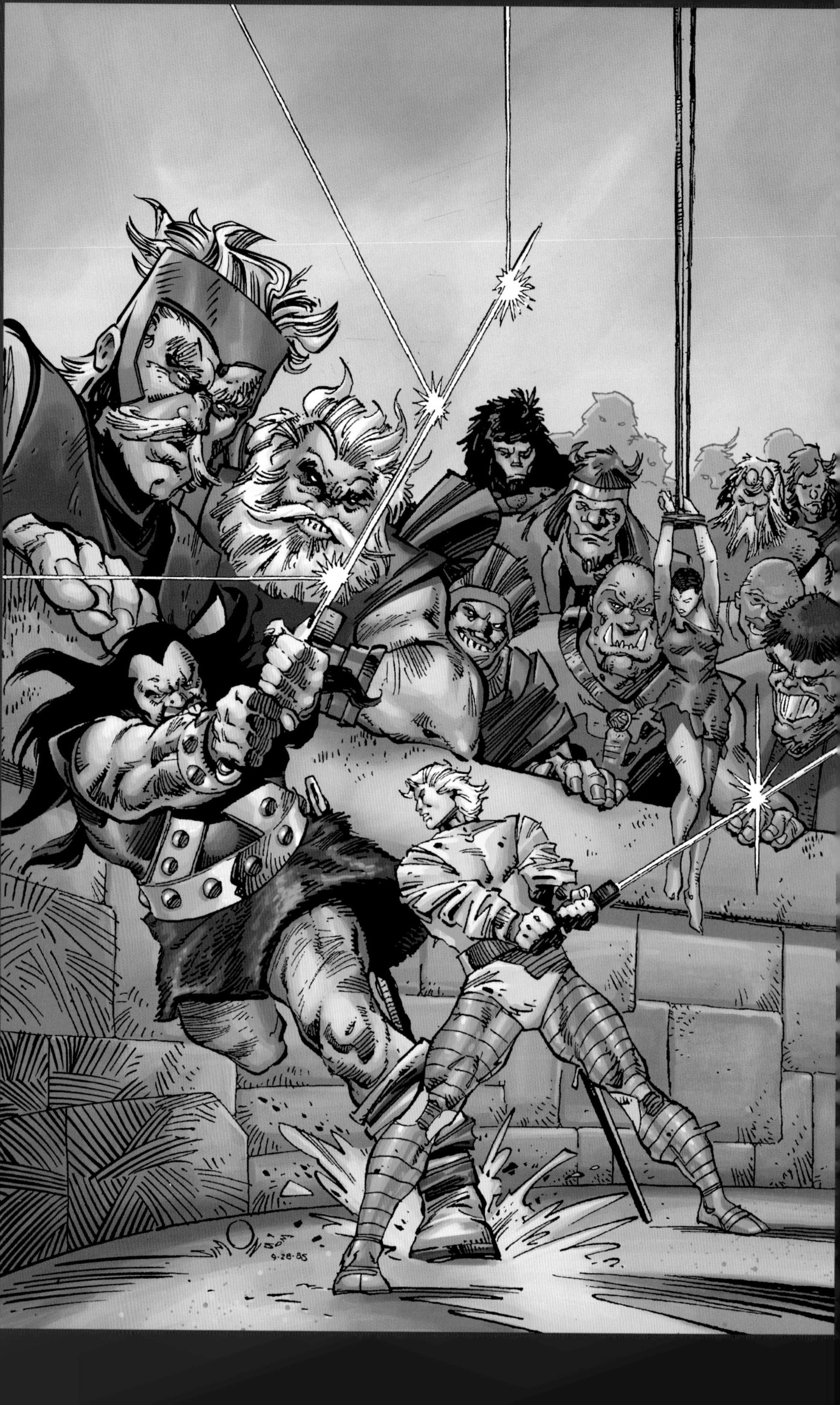